THE
OPPOSITE
LIFE

THE OPPOSITE LIFE

UNLOCKING
THE
MYSTERIES
OF
GOD'S
UPSIDE
DOWN
KINGDOM

ALEX SEELEY

W PUBLISHING GROUP

An Imprint of Thomas Nelson

Published in Nashville, Tennessee, by W Publishing, an imprint of Thomas Nelson.

Thomas Nelson titles may be purchased in bulk for educational, business, fund-raising, or sales promotional use. For information, please e-mail SpecialMarkets@ThomasNelson.com.

Any Internet addresses, phone numbers, or company or product information printed in this book are offered as a resource and are not intended in any way to be or to imply an endorsement by Thomas Nelson, nor does Thomas Nelson vouch for the existence, content, or services of these sites, phone numbers, companies, or products beyond the life of this book.

ISBN 978-0-7852-1613-1 (eBook)

Library of Congress Control Number: 2019901086

ISBN 978-0-7180-7510-1

Printed in the United States of America

19 20 21 22 23   LSC   10 9 8 7 6 5 4 3 2 1

To my Mother.

Thank you for never losing the fire.

You have shown me firsthand what it means
to keep going and to never give up. To always
speak truth in love no matter the cost.

I honor you and love you so very much.

ACKNOWLEDGMENTS

It takes a village to move a book from being an idea to actually resting on the shelf; therefore, I think it is only fitting to take a minute and thank those who were in my village and who made this book happen.

First, I want to thank my husband, Henry. He is my greatest champion in life. Thank you for being the voice of encouragement. Every time I said I can't, you said I can. Thank you for your continual support and the way you always release me to do what is in my heart. Also, thank you for the way you have led our family for the past two decades. You are my hero and the love of my life.

Thank you to my beautiful children, Holly and Taylor. Thank you for letting Mumma write these pages even when it meant eating takeout. I love you both more than anything in the whole world. You're my favorites.

A huge thank you needs to go to my beautiful friend Shelly Griffin—I honestly don't think I would have gotten this book over the line if it weren't for you. Thank you for your constant encouragement, your brilliant mind, your incredible patience, and your loyal friendship. Thank you for the way you serve and lead at the same time. Your friendship has meant more to me than you will ever know.

Thank you to Mia Dunnavant for being someone who always goes above and beyond. Thank you for all the love you have shown us as a family since the day we landed on US soil. You will always have a very special place in my heart. Your life is a true testament to God's beautiful story being outworked in you.

Danny Gokey, thank you for being who you are. You constantly show us how to serve and honor others. Your faithful example speaks volumes to those who are watching. Thank you for sharing your story.

Cameron Shadinger, thank you for being my Elisha. You have become a fierce warrior because you are an avid learner. Watching you navigate this journey with your family has been nothing short of stunning and beyond miraculous. I love how you speak so gently yet pray so fiercely. You are a sight to behold, and I am honored to have you in my life. Thank you for sharing your story.

Kara DiCarlo, to know you is to love you. From the moment I met you, I knew there was gold wrapped up inside you. Watching you grow into the mighty woman of God that you are has been so wonderful, and I look forward to seeing even more unfold. Thank you for sharing your vulnerable journey with others so that they may find hope and freedom.

To Debbie Wickwire, thank you for always challenging me to go higher by digging deeper. Forever grateful for your love and belief in me. You are a gift to this generation, and the generations still to come will be grateful for how you helped get such profound words into the hearts of so many.

Thank you Sam O'Neal for your amazing editing skills. You are a brilliant writer, and you have helped my process be an incredible experience. It has been so great working with you.

Last but certainly not least, thank you JESUS for being the ultimate example of what it looks like to move in the opposite spirit. You are perfect.

CONTENTS

CONTENTS

FOREWORD

I love people who are "deep wells"—those who you know have been through some rough stuff and navigated things that would have at best muddied or polluted other wells. These are the heroes who did the hard work to keep their waters pure and untainted. When this type of care is taken, it is not long before their deep wells become fountains of refreshment and life for others.

Alex Seeley is just such a well.

I first met Alex over a decade ago in the far away Land of Oz. I immediately loved this fiery Italian woman. Even though she was in a season of hardship and transition, she paused to pour encouragement and imagery into me, a stranger. It was Alex who first called me Sarah Connor—the protagonist of the Terminator movies—during a season in which I was intimidated by my own strength. Time passed. I watched as she and Henry left behind all they had known in Australia to come to the shores of America. She said they had won the citizenship lottery, but I think it was we Americans who actually won. They are a gift.

Alex and Henry came, prayed, and searched before planting their family in Nashville. It wasn't long before they were gathering with others in their home as they continued to seek God and pray into the needs of a city already overwhelmed by churches. They leaned into what seemed unlikely and even impossible: the idea of planting a church for the musicians that were away ministering over the weekends. The Belonging Co. was born out of their trembling obedience. It is a house of worship like no other.

I've had the privilege of watching their journey, and that is why I'm so glad Alex took the time to pen what she learned along the way. Each page of this book is more than typed words—they are weapons of love and life. With these hard won truths, Alex warns us that there is a very real Enemy who would love nothing more than to have us fight like him. Whenever we fall into playing the Enemy's game, he has already accomplished what he hoped for: division.

There is only one way to win. It is by embracing the Opposite Life. Where there is hate, we respond with love. When we are cursed, we respond with blessing. When we are treated like slaves, we respond as servants. Alex encourages us to fight each battle from heaven's vantage point. We don't wage war with earthly weapons but with weapons far more superior—weapons with eternal origins that pull down the enemy's strongholds and release the reality of God's kingdom realm.

> For though we walk in the flesh, we are not waging war according to the flesh. For the weapons of our warfare are not of the flesh but have divine power to destroy strongholds. We destroy arguments and every lofty opinion raised against the knowledge of God, and take every thought captive to obey Christ, being ready to punish every disobedience, when your obedience is complete. (2 Cor. 10:3–6 ESV)

Our broken earth longs for just this type of unveiling. It is time for us to remember who we are and respond as sons and daughters of the Most High God. There is a desperate longing for His goodness in the face of overwhelming anger, pain, and confusion.

The Opposite Life is a drink of living water in a dry and arid land.

—Lisa Bevere
New York Times bestselling author of
Without Rival and *Girls with Swords*

ONE MOVING IN THE OPPOSITE SPIRIT

When I was twenty-one years old, I was finally ready. Since the age of eleven, I'd dreamed of going into full-time ministry. But after high school my father had asked me to get a job before going to seminary, even if just for a year or so. I guess he wanted me to be sure I knew what I was doing, and maybe even have a few experiences in the marketplace so I would be certain ministry was my calling.

But after a couple of years of working as an administrative assistant at a law firm, I knew that administration was not my passion; people were. So I enrolled in Bible college. I was over-the-moon excited. I was eager to begin learning the deep truths of the Bible so that I could step into my God-given calling.

During this time, someone very close to me began to provoke

me in hurtful ways, cutting my heart deeply. For the sake of protecting that person's identity, I am going to call him Fred. He was not a Christian; in fact, he was quite averse to anything remotely related to church or ministry. Whenever we talked, he would tease me and call me derogatory names in an obvious attempt to get a reaction. But I always remained calm, because I felt like that was the Christian thing to do. I believed I was supposed to grin and bear it.

He was relentless in his pursuit to upset me, and one day his taunts escalated. Besides the usual name-calling, he said something that was unforgiveable and then finished the sentence with, "Who do you think you are, trying to become a pastor?" I finally lost my cool and let him have it. Uncontrollable anger burned inside of me. I yelled at him and cussed right back with fire in my tongue, wanting to hurt him as badly as he'd hurt me. I felt justified in my decision to fight back.

Later, as I was talking to my mum about it, I couldn't get past what had happened. And my heart hurt even further when she didn't take my side. How could she not see that I was justified to respond the way I had? Enough was enough, right?

"Don't you even care that he was rude to me?" I asked her.

That was when my very wise mum said, "Alex, who is the Christian in this scenario?"

"Well, I am, of course."

"Exactly," she said. "He doesn't know any better than to be insulting, to verbally attack you. However, you do. You could have walked away without saying a word. You need to forgive him and ask for his forgiveness for the things you said to him in anger."

I was stunned. But she wasn't finished.

"If you really want to be a minister of the gospel who practices what you preach, then you need to understand the principle of moving in the opposite spirit. Kindness would have disarmed the situation, because kindness is not what he was expecting from you. He was expecting anger, likely even goading you to see if he could get a reaction out of you, and he succeeded. You allowed his words to become personal instead of seeing him through the eyes of Jesus. Nothing he said to you should have had any bearing on who you are. Next time you find yourself in a similar situation, you need to show love to that person, even when they hurt you. That will change the atmosphere and give you authority over the situation."

Her advice seemed impossible to carry out. How could I forgive someone who continually hurt me? I honestly didn't want to forgive Fred, and I told her so.

So she went on. "It's true you can't do this by yourself. You need the Holy Spirit's help to forgive. Why don't you go find a quiet place and talk to God about it. Ask Him how you should respond."

Though I did pray, I didn't need to do so in order to figure things out—I already knew the answer. Jesus said in Luke 6, "Love your enemies, do good to those who hate you" (v. 27). And that's what I was called to do.

WHAT'S REALLY GOING ON

Living with a loving and forgiving heart can feel defeating. It seems as though the wicked get through life without a problem and

Christians are the ones who suffer. It seems as though the wicked don't get called out for their bad behavior while people of faith are called to a higher standard. It seems as though the wicked go unpunished while God's children are held accountable. It seems as though the wicked get the upper hand while the faithful take the heat.

This may be how you *feel*, but the truth is, the very opposite thing is taking place in the spiritual realm. What I learned from my mum that day was the importance of living according to the "opposite spirit." By this, I mean acting in a way that is contrary to what is expected in our world. The Holy Spirit living in us allows us to react positively, which is contrary to the negativity coming our way. As a result, we exchange generosity for greed. We exchange peace for stress. We exchange excellence for laziness. We exchange silence and wholesome words for gossip. Or in my specific case, I exchanged forgiveness and kindness for slander.

Since then, I've come to realize that when we move in the opposite spirit of what we naturally want to do in our flesh, we activate God to move on our behalf and fight the battle for us in the spiritual realm. Rather than fighting flesh and blood, we begin to war against the authorities and rulers of the spiritual realm over our lives (Eph. 6:12). We defeat the Enemy by doing things God's way, which is what the kingdom of God is all about. When faced with a situation, we should ask ourselves, "What would Jesus do?" Asking this question can yield miraculous results in our lives. Living in the opposite spirit enables us to live victoriously, with great power and abundance.

When we move in the opposite spirit on a consistent basis, we are storing credits in a heavenly bank account, so to speak. Every time we respond with love instead of reacting in anger, Jesus sees our choice and records it (Rev. 20:12), even if the person we are interacting with doesn't change. Our account builds over time, with interest, and offers a reward in this life and the life to come. What we sow, we will reap. And when we sow goodness in times of hardship, we will reap goodness. Luke 6:35 says it clearly: "But love your enemies, do good to them, and lend to them without expecting to get anything back. Then your reward will be great, and you will be children of the Most High." God rewards us when we move in the opposite spirit, and the reward will be far greater than anything we can imagine.

If we live life God's way, our lives will flourish. For those who oppose God's way, their lives will not flourish unless they repent and turn from their ways. Isaiah 55:7 says, "Let the wicked forsake their ways and the unrighteous their thoughts. Let them turn to the LORD, and he will have mercy on them." The bad guys never win in the end, but a repentant heart always does.

In my case, I didn't get justice—even after I apologized to Fred. But God brought a reward for my own heart. My response pleased the heart of God because I was reflecting His nature and not the nature of my flesh.

Fred continued to mock me and berate me for being a Christian. His insults often came out of nowhere and sometimes at the worst possible time in an attempt to throw me off my game. However, as I grew stronger in my faith and stood by my decision to see him with different eyes, I found that love was growing in my heart for him.

I found myself responding in love instead of reacting in offense. Over the next year, I saw him completely change his stance toward me. He stopped mocking me and started engaging in real conversations. He even began to seem interested in what I was pursuing.

I don't see Fred very often today, but when we do connect it's lovely. I have heard through the grapevine how much he respects my life. I have even had the opportunity to pray with him several times when he has been in crisis. Though it would appear he might not be living for God, his heart toward God has softened greatly, which is a miracle in itself.

LIVING OUT THE TRUTH

Imagine how the world could be impacted if followers of Jesus all moved in the opposite spirit to that which we find in our cultures. Imagine if Christians actually practiced what we are instructed to do in the Bible. Jesus spoke about how to move in the opposite spirit in Luke 6:

> But to you who are listening I say: Love your enemies, do good to those who hate you, bless those who curse you, pray for those who mistreat you. If someone slaps you on one cheek, turn to them the other also. If someone takes your coat, do not withhold your shirt from them. Give to everyone who asks you, and if anyone takes what belongs to you, do not demand it back. Do to others as you would have them do to you. . . . But love your

enemies, do good to them, and lend to them without expecting to get anything back. (vv. 27–31, 35)

"Love your enemies." That's a countercultural thought, I know, but the Bible is really clear on how we need to respond to our enemies. Still, it continues to astound me how, as Christians, we justify our actions and bend biblical truth to rationalize our responses. Also, we need to remember that our enemies are not always strangers. In fact, when Jesus speaks about loving our enemy in Matthew 5:44, the Greek translation for the word *enemy* used in this verse means our personal enemy. Our enemies aren't just the evil people we read about or watch on the news, but they can also be family members and people we thought were our friends.

As we live out the truth of the gospel, the results are staggering. It is not always easy to do, since our flesh is often screaming to do what *feels* right. But if we discipline our lives to obey the Word of God, we will gain a peace that transcends understanding and receive a reward from doing things God's way. And Scripture promises that when we obey, goodness and mercy will follow us all the days of our lives (Ps. 23:6).

Moving in the opposite spirit is one of the highest weapons of spiritual warfare in a Christian's arsenal, and when used consistently, it is a weapon of mass destruction to the Enemy. It displaces strongholds in the spirit realm over our lives and releases the angel armies to fight on our behalf. This, in turn, yields supernatural results in the natural realm. The rewards are priceless, because when we act in the opposite spirit against the Enemy, we receive a level of freedom, power, and authority the world cannot understand.

Moving in the opposite spirit has many benefits:

- We will receive any good that we do back from the Lord (Eph. 6:5–8).
- Wrath is forced to leave (Prov. 15:1).
- God hears our prayers (1 John 5:14).
- God vindicates us (Rom. 12:19).
- He supplies all our needs according to His riches (Phil. 4:19).
- We receive heavenly rewards for enduring in this life (Luke 6:22–23).
- We live in peace (2 Cor. 13:11).

LOOKING DIFFERENT

I truly believe that as followers of Jesus we are missing the point if we think memorizing scriptures and reciting them verbatim is the goal of our Christian walk. In our day-to-day lives, consistently practicing what we preach is what is important. Jesus is our greatest example. He studied and knew the Old Testament scriptures, but He also led a perfect life, and everything He did brought glory and honor to God. He introduced us to a new kingdom way of living, a way completely opposite of what feels natural. And His way yields supernatural results.

While studying the Gospels, I began to see that Jesus regularly asked His disciples to do the exact opposite of what people had done for generations. He asked them to live a life in which their spirit dictated their flesh, rather than their flesh dictating their spirit. As His followers, He asks the same of us. Living according to the Spirit is what makes us different and sets us apart from the world. The Christian lifestyle should stop people in their tracks. And as we live lives opposite to the world's way of interacting and responding, we can begin to turn the world upside down.

Jesus did this not by declaring war or fighting battles. He turned the world upside down and inside out by living and moving in the opposite spirit to the natural realm. He didn't follow the expected. He threw the natural things into chaos and caused people to see a different point of view. He acted in a completely foreign way to how most in His time did. He did so with such simplicity and kindness that even children could grasp these new concepts. He loved instead of hated. He gave instead of taking. He served instead of expecting to be served. He forgave instead of seeking revenge.

Imagine a world where we don't seek revenge when we get hurt but rather seek to bless instead. A world where the need to be right means less to us than the need to be in right relationships. A world where generosity is freely given with no strings attached just because we understand it is better to give than receive. A world where there is no insecurity or pride because we have discovered the secret that each and every human is loved and highly favored. A world where we live according to God's kingdom philosophy, and bless and serve all those around us as a result.

One of our world's driving needs is for retribution. If someone steals from you, then you are expected to prosecute him or her. If someone hits you on the cheek, you should punch him or her back. An eye for an eye, a tooth for a tooth. Sounds savage, doesn't it? When we are wronged, our immediate instinct is to get revenge. We want to cast blame and seek justice.

As the church, God calls us to live unlike the world. The apostle Peter wrote:

> Dear friends, I urge you, as foreigners and exiles, to abstain from sinful desires, which wage war against your soul. Live such good lives among the pagans that, though they accuse you of doing wrong, they may see your good deeds and glorify God on the day he visits us.
>
> Submit yourselves for the Lord's sake to every human authority: whether to the emperor, as the supreme authority, or to governors, who are sent by him to punish those who do wrong and to commend those who do right. For it is God's will that by doing good you should silence the ignorant talk of foolish people. (1 Pet. 2:11–15)

Another Bible translation says that we are "aliens and strangers" (NASB) in this world who are away from our eternal home. Here we are called foreigners, but we are commissioned to go *into* the world and make disciples, teaching them to obey what Jesus taught. We are to teach them God's way of doing things according to the kingdom of heaven.

If I'm honest, when I look over history and the way the global church has behaved on this earth, I see that we've often operated more like institutions of law and judgment rather than places of safety, acceptance, and love. Religion has too often focused more on the things it's against than on creating a place of refuge; it has facilitated more wars than peace. Is it any wonder why the world looks at the church and sees something God never intended it to look like? The gospel is meant to be conveyed in deeds, not just in words. Talk is cheap, but the gospel in action is priceless and has the ability to change the world.

As I read through the New Testament, I discovered that sinners loved hanging out with Jesus. If I were to ask sinners today whether they like hanging out with Christians, I'm afraid the answer would be no. We have become a body known for what we are against instead of what we stand for.

A friend once said to me, "Alex, everyone wants the real Jesus." And I believe this to be true. Jesus was kind and He was truthful. He never compromised His core beliefs, and yet everyone around Him was given an opportunity to be changed for the better.

Perhaps we as the church have missed our calling to follow Jesus' example with the message of the gospel. Rather than living an opposite life and changing the world, we've been filling up our time with knowledge from the Bible without going the next step of applying it to our everyday lives. We have been hearers of the Word but not doers of the Word (James 1:22). We have been listening but not applying the kingdom principles Jesus taught when He walked the earth.

Maybe this whole time we have overcomplicated things and are actually missing the point of the gospel. The gospel is "good news" but are we spreading good news or bringing bad news to our world? Maybe there is a way of life that will bring the greatest joy and reward and will allow us to live free and content to be all we were predestined to be. By living the opposite life, we begin to live as God intended His children to live: in harmony and unity, with power, abundance, and more blessing than we can contain. Maybe we can become the solution to the world's decaying problems. Maybe, just maybe, this opposite life has been the secret weapon all along.

GOD'S WAY OF DOING THINGS YIELDS A REWARD

Let's imagine for a moment we have been given the secret formula to a powerful and abundant life that promises blessing and favor. Not a perfect life, but a blessed life. Sometimes we equate material success as blessing but I'm talking about a blessed life full of peace and joy, something money can't buy. A life that sees the goodness of God in the land of the living. A life where our marriages are blessed, our children are blessed, and our careers and callings are blessed. I propose this formula exists, and that it is living according to the principles of the kingdom of God as laid out in the Bible and lived out by Jesus.

The kingdom of God is, at its core, God's way of doing things. In Isaiah 55:8, the Lord says, "For my thoughts are not your thoughts, neither are your ways my ways." God's ways are higher, and His thoughts are greater. Sometimes they don't make sense to us, but we can trust that His ways are perfect and only for our good. Because of His love for us, He sent His Son, Jesus, to earth to reveal the secret: life on God's terms is the very best way to live.

God's way of life never promises to be perfect or free of adversity, but He does promise that if you follow His principles, you will reap what you sow, you will not be in lack, you can overcome fear, and you will live an abundant and beautiful life. It will be a life full of freedom, joy, and love. A life where you can overcome every situation and live in peace. Peace! Isn't that what we all want? A beautiful life blessed on this side of eternity. So many Christians are hanging on by a thread until Jesus comes back so that they can finally live in paradise, but God promises an abundant life here on earth *now*.

Imagine with me a life filled with beauty, favor, and blessing. A harmonious life free of fear and anxiety. A life that promises happiness and joy when we follow the ways of God. It's possible. I'm living proof that the blessings of God are attainable even though I have gone through my fair share of trials and disappointments over my lifetime.

If you want to know the secret weapon to living life with supernatural power and abundance, then let me take you on a journey of doing things God's way. Let's see how this opposite way of life will change you for the better as you make daily decisions that will affect you and those around you in profound ways. This book is filled with real-life testimonies of ordinary people who decided to do things in the opposite realm. The result? Incredible miracles and blessings because they chose to align themselves with God's way—the kingdom way.

However, before we move on, I do need to warn you. If you

consider entering the mysterious realm of the opposite life, you will need to adjust your thinking and undergo a paradigm shift in your heart and mind, because living this way will go against your natural instincts. You will need to first know the One who created this kingdom way. Why? Because you cannot do it in your own strength. You need the supernatural strength that comes from salvation. When we encounter the unconditional love of Jesus and realize that it is by grace that we have been forgiven, everything about our lives should change for the better. Jesus promises that we become a new creation when we receive Him as Lord and Savior. The old is gone and the new way of doing things begins. Our eyes are open to a new way of living, and everything begins to change when these new ways are applied. Repentance is the entryway of this new life. To *repent* means to turn away and go in the opposite direction, back to our original design as sons and daughters of God.

This life of doing things in the opposite realm won't feel instinctual at first. But once you start renewing your mind with God's Word, listening to the voice of the Holy Spirit, and applying these new principles, you will see results that will turn your world upside down and inside out.

This life is not for the fainthearted. This life is for those who are bold and courageous. Jesus calls us to lay down our lives and pick up our cross in order to follow Him. For those who place their trust in a Being greater than themselves. A Being who created a perfect world that was destroyed through man's sin but is now redeemed because of His love for us when He sent His Son, who revealed what this opposite life of His kingdom could look like here on earth.

A life with Jesus is the one we all dream about but struggle to find the road map to. Or perhaps our struggle is actually following the instructions on the road map. It's a life that leads to blessings upon blessings, not just in this life, but also in the one to come— eternal blessings.

At the end of each chapter there is a challenge to help you begin your journey of moving in the opposite realm. Answer the questions with honesty and pray for God to help you as you read through the pages of this book. I believe we are not to just be hearers of the Word but doers of the Word. I promise you that if you choose to step out and take these challenges, you will see incredible results.

Get ready to have your thoughts challenged and your heart rerouted into new places. At times you will likely feel scared to jump off into the unknown. Perhaps following God's instructions will feel foolish or like a waste of time, but once you discover that this opposite life brings forth success and favor, the kind you could only dream about, you will wonder why it took you so long to find it.

CHALLENGE

Jesus asked the disciples to come and follow Him. They left their old way of life and everything that was familiar. Today, He is inviting you to do the same and begin the journey of moving in the opposite spirit. Make a commitment to undergo the paradigm shift. The opposite life will yield supernatural results. It has been the secret weapon all along.

TWO | THE OPPOSITE CHOICE

They say that opposites attract, and that's often true in marriage. Who we think we want in our lives is not always who we need, and sometimes we need the exact opposite of what we thought was best for us.

That was the case for me.

When I was growing up, I believed that opposites attract on a physical level. I've got dark hair and hazel eyes, so naturally I was attracted to men with blond hair and blue eyes. And tall too—or at least taller than me. And I always pictured my children with fair hair and blue eyes.

But as a twenty-three-year-old still waiting for my knight in shining armor, I didn't see any blond-haired, blue-eyed Vikings among my friends or in my community.

There was Henry, though. We'd met three years earlier when we volunteered as youth team leaders at our church and quickly became best friends. I knew from the moment I met him that he was a great guy, and I had thought that whoever married this guy was going to be blessed, but it never occurred to me that I would be the one to marry him.

Henry and I had the perfect setup for a great friendship. He often came to me with his girl problems, and I went to him with my boy problems. But I had no attraction at all for Henry because he was not what I had imagined—he had green eyes and brown hair, and we were the same height.

Then, about two years into our friendship, something changed. I found myself thinking about Henry more and more. I wanted to spend more time in his company. I noticed him more, and I would catch myself wanting him to notice me.

I remember the moment everything finally clicked in my mind. We were practicing a worship set, and I realized I was *staring* at Henry—outright staring at him in the middle of a praise song—and I really liked what I was seeing! The physical attraction shocked me to the very core of my being.

Oh my goodness, I thought, *why am I finding Henry attractive? This can't be happening!* I kept trying to convince myself the attraction wasn't real. I would remind myself that I did love Henry, but just as a friend. Nothing more.

But part of me knew something undeniable was happening. We had begun working together on staff at church, and every time I went to work and collected my mail, I could tell whether Henry had arrived before me from the smell of his cologne. Each time I recognized his familiar scent, my heart leapt with excitement. *He's here!*

I kept these feelings to myself because I was too scared to utter a word to anyone. I knew if I told Henry and he didn't feel the same way about me, it could ruin our friendship. And we worked together, which would make things awkward for everyone if there was tension between us.

I was in a quandary of emotion and found myself praying about the situation throughout each day. *God, You know the desires of my heart, and I think I can only be happy with a man who has blond hair and blue eyes, because You know how much I have always wanted children with blue eyes and fair-colored hair.*

I find it hilarious now as I look back over my thought processes, but how many times do we become fixated on what we think is best and end up missing God's gift right in front of us?

I continued in earnest dialogue with God, admittedly frustrated because I had an ideal of what I thought I needed in my life—and Henry was not it. Why was God giving me the complete opposite of what I wanted? It was like saying you want to serve God, but when He says, "Go to the uttermost part of the earth," you freak out because that's completely outside your comfort zone.

This idea of being with Henry was completely not what I had imagined. It took me a while to accept the reality that maybe my destiny was with Henry. My heart felt drawn toward the idea, but I still struggled to accept that Henry was the man I was supposed to be with. How could I know I wouldn't want someone else later? Was he my only option? I prayed and asked God to confirm that being with Henry was what was best. When I received five different confirmations in answer to those prayers, I gave in. Then I waited patiently for Henry to pursue me.

Fast-forward over a year because Henry took his sweet time realizing he liked me too. When he finally asked me to be his girlfriend, I said yes and went home floating on a cloud. I couldn't wait to tell my parents!

God's ways are higher than our ways, and His thoughts are much greater than our thoughts. I could have missed one of the very best things that has happened to me if I had followed my own desires. Henry may not have looked like the husband I expected as a young girl, but God knew what I needed. And over the years I've become even more convinced Henry is the exact person I needed in my life—and he's the person I still need after twenty years of marriage. Little did I know that he would also be the most incredible father to our two miracle children, Holly and Taylor.

Because I chose to lay down my preconceived ideas of what I *thought* would make me happy, I not only married the greatest human ever created, but I also get to serve the Lord alongside him in ways I never could have imagined.

I believe God gave me more than I deserved and blessed me beyond words because I chose to trust God even when it didn't make sense at the time. I chose His kingdom way over my way. Even though this road to marriage was not easy, our relationship has been blessed for the past twenty years. (And by the way, I love those green eyes!) And you wouldn't believe it, but both our children have fair hair and blue eyes!

God's ways often don't look the way we imagined them, but He surprises us over and above all we could ever dream. As Ephesians 3:20–21 says, "Now to him who is able to do immeasurably more than all we ask or imagine, according to his power that is at work within us, to him be glory in the church and in Christ Jesus throughout all generations, for ever and ever! Amen."

JESUS: THE OPPOSITE OF WHAT THEY EXPECTED

Israel had waited for hundreds of years for the Redeemer to come and save them from bondage. They were imagining the King of all kings coming from the throne of heaven in a blaze of glory to rescue them from their tyrant oppressors.

Isaiah 9:6 says the government would be carried on His shoulders, so the Jewish nation believed their king was coming to deliver them from the Roman Empire and rule over them. But as we know now, Jesus came into this world completely opposite to the way they expected Him to come. They expected Him to fight the political system of their day. They expected an earthly deliverance. They expected Him to act like an earthly king.

Yet from the very beginning of Jesus' life, everything was different. Even Jesus' arrival looked nothing like their expectations. He came in seed form, supernaturally impregnated by the Holy Spirit to a virgin girl named Mary. Jesus was born in a stable in Bethlehem, not a royal palace. Not exactly the grandest entrance for a king. Not very kingdom-esque.

If that wasn't bad enough, and if that wasn't far enough removed from royal expectations, Jesus was raised in the humble surroundings of a carpenter's home. And by a man who was not His biological father.

Joseph, who was betrothed to Mary, initially tried to come up with a way out of this arrangement because he was fully aware he was not the father of the child growing in Mary's womb. Can you imagine what Joseph was going through and what his thought process may have been? Can you imagine the cultural and spiritual weight he must have felt? His fiancée was claiming the Holy Spirit had supernaturally planted the seed of God into her womb. Hold on a minute. This could not be the Messiah prophesied about for thousands of years, could it? An illegitimate baby born to a virgin (Isa. 7:14)? Impossible!

God is always faithful to show up in impossible situations and reveal truth. One night, as Joseph was still trying to decide if he should break off the engagement or marry Mary, an angel visited him. "An angel of the Lord appeared to him in a dream and said, 'Joseph son of David, do not be afraid to take Mary home as your wife, because what is conceived in her is from the Holy Spirit'" (Matt. 1:20).

Despite the angel's reassurance, Joseph still had to agree to raise this boy. With that came responsibility for all three of them, and all the baggage of this unbelievable scenario. The people in their community were not going to believe their story, so if Joseph was going to follow the Lord's command, he had to move in the opposite spirit of what felt comfortable; he had to trust God. Moving forward meant he would risk being ridiculed and mocked. Even so, he obeyed and chose to stand by Mary's side, thus becoming the father of the Messiah, even when God's plan didn't make sense. But God's ways often don't make any sense. As Isaiah 55:8 says, "'For my thoughts are not your thoughts, neither are your ways my ways,' declares the LORD."

To the world, it looked crazy that the Holy Spirit would supernaturally place a seed into the womb of a teenager, but to Mary and Joseph it was a miracle. They partnered with that miracle even though they had been given every opportunity to say no. Aren't you glad they both said yes?

As the Lord did with Joseph, God may ask us to do things completely opposite to what we ever dreamed or imagined. He may require us to live in a way that makes no sense whatsoever to the average person in our surrounding culture, or even to us. We have to make a choice to partner with His ways and His methods, even when doing that can mean being misunderstood or risking our reputation. Aligning ourselves with God allows us to partner with Him to fulfill the plans He has for us.

JESUS: A PIONEER OF THE UNLIKELY

Jesus was the pioneer of doing all things opposite. He was a master of living in a realm opposite of humanity's. He came to declare a new world order, and following His teachings is the way into this heavenly kingdom realm.

While on earth, Jesus taught the people how to behave as citizens of His kingdom. Can you imagine trying to change the mind-set of the Jewish nation, of a people who had been following the laws of the Old Testament for thousands of years? However, Jesus wasn't coming to abolish these laws—He was coming to fulfill them.

Finally, every prophetic word spoken about a new kingdom and its king was being fulfilled, and the Messiah they had been waiting for was walking right in front of them in the person of Jesus. But the kingdom that Jesus talked about didn't sound like the one they had been hoping for. This kingdom realm would not free the Jews from the oppression of the Roman Empire; rather, it would free them from an eternal separation from God.

JESUS: THE DESPISED KING

As we have discussed, many missed out on experiencing the Messiah because He didn't look like the king they had imagined. Perhaps they were expecting someone like Solomon, Saul, or David. They expected Him to be good-looking and regal and strong. Yet God chose to reveal His Son in a package people weren't naturally attracted to. Therefore, many dismissed Him. They didn't look beneath the surface to see the anointing He carried.

The people of Jesus' day could have been better informed about His coming if they had paid more careful attention to God's Word. Isaiah 53:2–3 says:

He grew up before him like a tender shoot,
and like a root out of dry ground.
He had no beauty or majesty to attract us to him,
nothing in his appearance that we should desire him.
He was despised and rejected by mankind,
a man of suffering, and familiar with pain.
Like one from whom people hide their faces
he was despised, and we held him in low esteem.

How many times have we done the same thing when someone doesn't look the way we think they should? We may ignore those who are less fashionable or less attractive according to our standards. We don't take the time to discover the quality of a person based on their heart and character and worth as a child of God. As a result, I think many of us have missed out on discovering true gold in a friendship or a relationship.

It breaks my heart to think Jesus was dismissed because, as the Scriptures state, He didn't look attractive enough. He was unimpressive to His culture. It breaks my heart to consider I may have rejected Him too if I had lived during His time. In my immaturity I have dismissed people because they looked different from me. I have overlooked those who required too much effort to understand their worth. I am so glad that over the years God has challenged me to always search beneath the surface. I truly have discovered some of the finest treasures in people by doing so.

John the Baptist, who was Jesus' forerunner, saw Jesus for who He was. John kept declaring to all who would hear, "Repent, for the kingdom of heaven has come near" (Matt. 3:2). He didn't see someone too tender to rule. He didn't see someone who wasn't cool enough or regal enough to become king. To John, Jesus' appearance couldn't discredit the truth of who He was. He was a king.

Somewhat ironically, notice that God chose someone completely opposite of what society might expect as the messenger to announce the coming of the Messiah. John the Baptist lived in the wilderness, in the desert. He wore camel hair as clothing and ate a diet of dried locusts and wild honey. Let's face it; he sounds weird. Yet God chose him to introduce Jesus and this new kingdom. Not someone we would consider a great PR choice, right?

For those attuned to the opposite life, though, something compelled them to come to the desert in droves to listen to John. The Bible tells us that many were saved and baptized by him (Matt. 3:6). We often think we can make a difference by doing things the same way they've always been done, but I think sometimes the world needs to see and experience something different in order to take notice.

JESUS: THE HUMBLE SERVANT

Jesus immediately set the stage for the opposite ways of the kingdom by the way He began His ministry. He humbled Himself by asking John the Baptist to baptize Him in water (Matt. 3:13–15). Jesus was God, without sin, and He had no need for cleansing or repentance, yet He asked to be baptized by a mere mortal. This just blows my mind.

If Jesus came today, we might expect that media outlets would be alerted, a huge launch party would be organized, and a press kit would be issued that would describe all the accolades and connections that made Jesus great. But no, that is not what Jesus would do. That was not the way He announced His kingdom. He came as a servant to be our example for what it means to go low, in order that God would be raised up.

What seems insignificant to man is often profound in God's kingdom. Jesus identified Himself with the sinful people He came to serve. In contrast, men and women tend to think they are better than the people they are serving. We elevate ourselves out of false pride and insecurity and are focused on needing others to serve us in all occasions. I have to admit, even in our churches we sometimes create a hierarchy when, in fact, we are all in need of mercy and grace. Yet when I look at Jesus, I see Him always serving, not demanding service for Himself.

Jesus was the Word made flesh according to the gospel of John (1:14). He was there in the beginning when God created the heavens and the earth. And now He had come to earth to save what was lost. But instead of lording His power over people, He humbled Himself and made Himself of no reputation, eventually enduring the cross. He served and poured Himself out as an offering to us unto death. This was definitely opposite of what anyone had in mind when they imagined a Messiah coming to earth to save it. No wonder He was so misunderstood and despised by so many.

THE KINGDOM BLUEPRINT UNFOLDED

Jesus began His ministry at the age of thirty. He was baptized and then immediately entered into the wilderness where, for forty days, He was tempted by the Enemy. Overcoming those long days of multiple temptations accomplished what God intended—demonstrating Jesus' authority to do the work He'd been called to do.

After returning to Galilee, Jesus began teaching publicly, and the people noticed there was something different about Him. Still, they couldn't reconcile who He was in the natural world. And they couldn't fathom that He could be the Messiah.

Luke 4:16–20 says:

He went to Nazareth, where he had been brought up, and on the Sabbath day he went into the synagogue, as was his custom. He stood up to read, and the scroll of the prophet Isaiah was handed to him. Unrolling it, he found the place where it is written:

"The Spirit of the Lord is on me,
because he has anointed me
to proclaim good news to the poor.
He has sent me to proclaim freedom for the prisoners
and recovery of sight for the blind,
to set the oppressed free,
to proclaim the year of the Lord's favor."

Then he rolled up the scroll, gave it back to the attendant and sat down. The eyes of everyone in the synagogue were fastened on him.

Those in the synagogue that day were caught off guard by the way He presented Himself and were "amazed at the gracious words that came from his lips" (v. 22). They all sat in awe and wonder. But then someone asked, "Isn't this Joseph's son?" (v. 22). After Jesus chastised the people for their unbelief, the atmosphere in the room changed. They became furious when they heard Jesus speak of Himself as the Messiah and wanted to kill Him.

It was there in Nazareth that they first rejected Jesus. One wonders what questions had filled their minds as He began to speak. Did they wonder what His territory expansion plans were? Which prominent leaders and important men would He appoint to be on His government team? Where would His hub of power be located? Did He have a plan to overthrow the Romans? But was this the kind of information that made up Jesus' first speech to the people He would govern? Not at all. His kingdom rule was opposite of what they expected. It went above the natural laws of the land and entailed orders around issues of the heart. He was working on the kingdom *within* mankind.

Jesus was not what anyone expected in the way He came down from heaven, in the way He began His leadership through serving and submission, or in the nature of His role—and yet many were completely drawn to Him. There was something about this man that was different from all the other prophets and rabbis.

UNLOCKING THE MYSTERIES

In the pages ahead we will begin to unpack this opposite life that Jesus came to show us. Each chapter is titled with an issue that we will encounter at some point in our lives, such as facing fear, wanting revenge, struggling with pride, feeling weak, and dealing with doubt. Then we'll unlock the mystery of how to overcome these issues by moving in the opposite spirit to how we might naturally respond.

It takes faith to both believe that Jesus Christ is the Son of God and receive Him as Lord and Savior. Many in Jesus' day missed it because He did not look like they thought He should. They looked with their natural eyes instead of using their spiritual eyes. What about you?

Sometimes Jesus presents Himself to us in a form that seems obscure and the complete opposite of what we are expecting. If we are not paying attention, we can miss the very best thing that will change our lives for the better. Jesus is trying to help us look at things in a new way. He offers us a paradigm shift so we can view the world and everything in it through His eyes, thus seeing the best and yielding the best results. His kingdom blueprint is a masterful plan.

CHALLENGE

What in your life looks contrary to the way you expected it? Don't dismiss or ignore what may seem opposite to how you hoped it would be. Ask the Lord to open your eyes to see what He says about the situation or person. It could be a blessing in disguise.

THREE

DEATH VS. LIFE

"Whoever wants to be my disciple must deny themselves and take up their cross daily and follow me.
For whoever wants to save their life will lose it, but
whoever loses their life for me will save it."

—Luke 9:23–24

When I was eleven years old, I prayed a prayer to invite Jesus into my heart. But it wasn't until the age of twenty-one that I came to the end of doing things *my* way. I chose to surrender my life to Jesus and make Him my Lord and Savior, drawing a line in the sand; there was no turning back. Prior to that, I stood with one foot in the world and one foot in church. But I realized that position wasn't working.

In order to follow Jesus, I had to lay down my whole life and die to my will and agenda. I needed to place my entire life in God's hands. I experienced the revelation that true repentance requires a death of my old nature; the result would be a resurrection of my new nature in Christ. This meant I needed to die to what I thought made me happy.

Even though doing that was hard at first, I found true life and fulfillment! I realized I could breathe without fear and insecurity. I saw things from a new perspective. I felt awe and wonder in the simplest things. I found a love so beautiful that nothing else could compare or satisfy like Jesus!

But I also learned that true discipleship meant a *lifestyle* of dying to self. I began to better understand Romans 12:1: "Offer your bodies as a living sacrifice, holy and pleasing to God—this is your true and proper worship." This is the lifestyle of a follower of Christ. We die in order to live.

You may be breathing, but are you truly living?

DEATH AND RESURRECTION OF DREAMS

In 2010 I was thirty-seven years of age, and I had been serving Jesus in vocational ministry for sixteen years. I had seen many good things manifest in my life as I continued to obey Him, and I had reached the point in my ministry life that others would have seen as the pinnacle. Henry and I were in a thriving church and doing incredible things for His kingdom. I was traveling with my husband, who was at the peak of his ministry and vocation as a worship leader.

We were doing all of this while living in beautiful Melbourne, Australia, and we thought life couldn't get any better. Then God dropped a simple thought into our hearts about moving to the United States. I was like, *What do You mean, God?* I wrestled with this idea for over two years, but it would not go away.

In 2012, after many confirmations and the miracle of receiving permanent residency in the United States, we left our family and friends and sold everything we owned. We moved eight thousand miles to the other side of the world to Nashville, Tennessee, with no idea of what would happen next, with nothing but a few suitcases and the presence of God. I thought we were entering the "promised land," but little did I know it was going to be a season where I had to die. Little did I know He was calling out my half-baked existence once again.

I was thirty-nine years old when we moved. I'd thought most of my dreams and the desires of my heart had come to fruition by this point, and that my life was secure and settled. Now I felt as if I'd been sent in the opposite direction, back into the desert of Nothingness, USA, and left for dead! I felt forgotten and abandoned by God.

I wrestled with God and found myself asking Him, *Why does it feel like I need to keep doing this death thing over and over again?* I thought surely by now I had done all the dying I needed to do.

I didn't literally die, of course, but God was exposing the motives for some of my dreams—and those did need to die. I didn't *really* understand what that meant until I laid it all on the altar as a sacrifice to the Lord that year of my life, until I surrendered every desire to Christ.

I was unaware that those dreams and visions I had for my life at that point were self-centered. Even though they were God dreams, I was at the center of attention instead of God. They had been about my platform and my influence, all hidden under the guise of "making God famous." It makes me cringe even writing that, but it was true.

When we moved to the States, I remember feeling a sense of accomplishment because we had obeyed the voice of God and had given up everything for Him. I was convinced that step of faith was enough to open the door of our future, but I was sadly mistaken. After being in Nashville for a few months, I found myself disappointed that God had not rolled out the red carpet for us to walk into our destiny. I expected opportunities in vocational ministry to open up. Not only did they not open for me, I couldn't even get a job in retail!

Stepping into the promised land was the easy part, but having to step up and take possession of it was another story. I resonated with Joshua and Caleb. Just because they entered the promised land as God instructed them didn't mean they had possession of it. They had to fight some battles and slay some giants before they could take dominion over the land and claim it as their own.

It was the same for our family. We stepped into our new

promised land, but the battles and giants I had to face were ever-present. And they were mostly those related to my own dreams and myself. I knew I had to die to them if I was going to have a full life.

I had been stripped of everything: my friends, my family, my career, and our finances. But it was at that point, with tears rolling down my cheeks and with the very real thought that I might never see my dreams realized, that I knew I had to trust God and surrender it all at the altar. I had to make the decision that it was okay if I never picked up another microphone to preach the Word of God. I had to be okay with the idea of no longer serving as a leader. I had to die to the dreams of influencing my generation through books or speaking. I placed my heart's longings on the altar. Lying facedown on my carpet, I remember saying, "Jesus, if all I have is You, then You are more than enough." I sowed surrender and trusted God to do what He thought was best for my life.

That's a scary and vulnerable place to be, but it's necessary for God to do what He wants to do in and through us for His glory. What happened that day on the carpet in my bedroom marked me for life. All of my motives died, along with my dreams, and I received the most priceless gift. I realized Jesus was more than enough in my life, and all that came after that was what God had predestined for me. That was all I wanted.

I had died to my own desires. I wasn't concerned with my career in ministry anymore. I didn't care what people thought about me anymore. All I cared about was being in right relationship with Jesus. All I wanted was fulfillment in just being with Him, not *doing* things for Him.

The beautiful part of this story is that from that moment on, I began to serve people just because I loved them, not because I was getting paid to love them. I began studying Scripture not because I had to preach a sermon, but because I wanted to know more about my Father in heaven. I began to look at life with a completely different lens. I truly discovered so much beauty and freedom.

Before I knew it, I was sharing out of the overflow of my heart every week in the basement of our home with people who were coming from all over Nashville to encounter the presence of God. I became more fruitful in serving God in this season than in my previous season in Australia. And now, after each step of obedience, God has given me the opportunity to lead a church in Nashville called The Belonging Co. In my wildest dreams I never would have thought it was possible. After sowing in the secret place for years, I was beginning to see the harvest being reaped in public. Death brought me life in so many unexpected ways.

DEATH OF SELF

God is jealous for our hearts and wants us yielded to Him not because He is a narcissist, but because He is a loving Father who desires to fulfill our purpose at the appointed time. The perfect time is usually when the gift in our lives does not make us famous but brings *Him* glory. We need to realize that anything we place above God is an idol—even perhaps our God-given dreams. And we need to lay down the things we have exalted above God and put it at the foot of the cross.

Jesus humbled Himself and took on the likeness of man and became obedient to the point of death on the cross. Therefore, God also exalted Him and gave Him the name which is above every name (Phil. 2:7–9). So how much more do we need to die in order for the purpose and destiny on our lives to reveal the glory of God? Jesus never came to be famous. He came to earth for the sole purpose of destroying the work of the Enemy, so that we could be reconciled back to the Father and reveal the glory of God. It was never about Him; it was always about us.

Jesus knew death on every level, not just physically. As fully God yet still fully man, He died to people's acceptance. "He was despised and rejected by mankind, a man of suffering, and familiar with pain" (Isa. 53:3). He died to a life of worldly affluence and wealth (He had no home, no place to rest His head). He died to His friends' opinions of Him (Judas betrayed Him, and Peter denied Him). He died to being validated and applauded. He died to being understood. "He made Himself of no reputation, taking the form of a bondservant, and coming in the likeness of men. . . . He humbled Himself and became obedient to the point of death, even the death of the cross" (Phil. 2:7–8 NKJV). He died to His own will and submitted to the Father's will. He died to fitting in. He died to a life of normality and ease and rest. He died on every level so that we could live.

Every dream has to die before it can be resurrected into its God-ordained purpose. Jesus said in John 12:24–25, "Very truly I tell you, unless a kernel of wheat falls to the ground and dies, it remains only a single seed. But if it dies, it produces many seeds. Anyone who loves their life will lose it, while anyone who hates their life in this world will keep it for eternal life." In our finite thinking, that sounds so devastating. Letting our dreams die feels painful, like grieving a loss, and we're sent into the stages of grief. We experience sadness, anger, and doubt, questioning God in the midst of our pain. We think God is punishing us or withholding from us during this death phase.

But dying is not final in God's kingdom; it is actually the pathway to life. So many of us don't want to die because we think we'll miss out. We think someone else is going to take up the mantle meant for us if we lay down that dream. I've come to realize it's only when we allow God to take us through the death process that we will finally discover what the true meaning of life is.

How does letting something go and embracing death produce life? Letting go and dying to yourself and your dreams is hard because it requires trust that God is not going to disappoint you and leave you for dead. God wants your heart to desire Him—true life—more than you desire the dream. It doesn't make sense in our natural mind, but the shift does something in the spirit realm. If we want to live a life of supernatural power and abundance, then we must first be willing to lay down our lives and dreams. If our dreams are from God, they will be resurrected back to life, producing much fruit and bringing Him glory. If God were never to do another thing for us in this lifetime, He has already done more than we deserve. This is the posture in which we must live. Grateful. The rest is just a bonus.

THE LAW OF SOWING AND REAPING

A seed has to die first before it can multiply. This is an age-old principle that's been true since the beginning of time.

Every seed carries within it a blueprint, so to speak. It already has all the information and instruction it will need once it is buried in the soil. There is massive potential in every seed, but unless it is buried and dies, it will never produce what it was predestined for.

Whatever has been designed inside that seed is what it shall become. If you plant an apple tree seed, you will not get anything but an apple tree. And so it is with us. If we sow anger, we will reap an anger tree. If we sow peace, we will reap a peace tree and eat of its fruit.

Inside each and every one of us is the DNA of what we are to become. I have learned that just because we have the potential to grow into our design doesn't mean that growth will automatically occur. For instance, God's predestined plan for your life doesn't just magically appear at the appointed time. We have to go through a process just like a seed does. A seed doesn't become a tree by sitting on the windowsill of a kitchen; it must be buried and it must die while being hidden for it to multiply and grow into the tree that it was predestined to be. That takes time.

Jesus makes it clear that we need to die before we can live (Rom. 6:8, 8:13; Luke 9:23–24). We need to be born again—not literally, but spiritually. The same goes for our destiny. We don't die physically and rise from the dead, but our flesh must die so that our spirit can come alive. Then we can begin to live from the new creation rather than the old man with a sinful nature.

LIFE FROM DEATH

There are a number of lessons we can learn about the opposite life when it comes to true living.

1. We must die if we are to live.

Jesus said, "I tell you the truth, unless you are born again, you cannot see the Kingdom of God" (John 3:3 NLT).

There is no entry into this spiritual life without first dying to our old life. We are not able to work out our own righteousness. If we have faith in ourselves, that faith must die. If we think it's about us and our gifts and talents, then this idea must die. It is not our good works that gain our righteousness, but instead His righteousness is given to us when we choose to surrender our lives. We then gain His life in us. Charles Spurgeon said it like this: "You must be slain by the sword of the Spirit before you can be made alive by the breath of the Spirit."[1]

2. We must surrender everything in order to keep anything.

In John 12:25, Jesus says, "He who loves his life will lose it" (NKJV).

What does this mean for us? It means we can't have a spiritual life with hope, joy, peace, and abundance until we surrender everything in exchange for His everything. Sometimes it looks like we haven't gained anything. But we will discover that as we surrender

---

1 Charles Haddon Spurgeon, *Talks to Farmers* (Auckland, New Zealand: Floating Press, 1889, 2013), 63.

our will—our rebellious heart that wants what it wants in its own way, and our pride that says we can do everything on our own—we gain a life that gives us more fulfillment than we could ever imagine. Surrender is the pathway to promotion, but it must come from our heart and not our head. Our surrender must be complete, and we have to realize that whatever we are giving up may never come back. In essence, we are saying Jesus is enough.

3. We must lose ourselves in order to find ourselves.

Jesus taught in John 12:25, "He who hates his life in this world will keep it for eternal life" (NKJV).

We must give up living for ourselves in order to truly discover who we are. We are all so busy trying to find ourselves by looking inside ourselves. But we will always come up short in discovering who we are because we are too busy holding on to who we think we are instead of who He says we are.

We will only find ourselves when we give ourselves away. The person who lives for himself or herself doesn't ever truly live. But when you live for others and for God, you find the truest version of yourself and the best quality of life. The Bible tells us that it is much better to give than receive (Acts 20:35). This has been true in my life. I have discovered the abundance of who I am as I have given myself wholeheartedly to God and to others. "There is no way of finding yourself in personal joy like losing yourself in the joy of others," Charles Spurgeon said.[2]

---

2 Spurgeon, *Talks to Farmers*, 64.

FATHER ABRAHAM

If we wish to achieve great purpose and do something that changes the world, we must surrender ourselves. Only then can we gain the heart of God and serve Him with all we have. Only then will we be all that God created us to be.

The Old Testament figure Abraham knew this well. Abraham was given a promise that he would be the father of many nations, yet there was a problem: he and his wife were old—like, really old. In fact, Sarah was barren and had long since given up on the idea of becoming a mother. But God promised they would conceive and bear a son who would be the first seed of His chosen people.

Abraham waited twenty-five years for this promise to come to pass. When the promised son, Isaac, arrived, we can only imagine how excited Abraham must have been. God had fulfilled His promise. But then, some years later, God asked Abraham to sacrifice Isaac, his beloved son, the one on whom the promise of descendants as numerous as the stars rested.

Hold on a minute! Sacrifice the son he had waited twenty-five years for? This seems ludicrous. This was the opposite of what God had promised, right? But God's ways are so much higher than our ways. God did not want Isaac to die, but He did want to test Abraham's heart and ask the questions, *Will you trust Me? And am I first in your life?*

As Abraham surrendered Isaac back to God, God saw his heart, and at that moment God connected with Abraham in a very deep and personal way. God affirmed that Abraham loved Him more than anything else. Abraham's heart was open to whatever God asked, even if it looked like the death of his promise. If Isaac had to die in order for God's promise to come true, Abraham trusted God without having to understand His ways.

Then the most miraculous thing happened. Abraham *did* become the father of many nations. God provided a ram so that Isaac was spared. And the seed that was willing to die in him multiplied to a vast number that is still growing today.

God doesn't ask us to die so that He can take away from us. God asks us to die to the flesh so that our Spirit man will arise and live as a new creation in Christ and live by the fruit of the Spirit (Gal. 5:16–26).

CHALLENGE

Ask the Lord what it is that you need to die to. When you know what it is, yield that seed into the hands of the Lord. If it is from God, it will produce a harvest beyond your wildest dreams.

FOUR

MASTER VS. SERVANT

"Whoever wants to become great among you must be your servant, and whoever wants to be first must be your slave—just as the Son of Man did not come to be served, but to serve, and to give his life as a ransom for many."

—Matthew 20:26–28

I believe God predestined every one of us with an amazing purpose and destiny to fulfill during our lifetimes. Sometimes we can feel guilty for wanting to do and be something great, but we need to understand that it is not arrogant to know who you are in Christ. Actually, it's quite the opposite. It's our responsibility.

When we know how truly great we are in Christ, allowing the process of greatness to take place in our lives becomes much easier. But before this greatness can be revealed, there is usually a season of serving someone or something that helps develop our character. And then, when we experience the greatness God has for us, instead of being crushed under the weight of that greatness, our character has been built to sustain it.

Many people in the current generation seem to want to be great for no reason except fame itself. And they want it now. They are becoming a generation that has no time for the process of refining and serving, because that is just boring. But Jesus said that in order to become great we must be servants. In other words, He was saying we must first lay down our own agendas and serve, allowing the process to bring true greatness out of us. He's after His glory reflected in our lives, not shallow fame. The greatness given to you is not actually about you; the greatness inside of you is about other people. And servanthood is the pathway to true greatness.

There is something significant about an apprentice season of service to another person's vision before ever stepping into your own. This has been true in my own life and the lives of many other men and women of influence. For example, Malcolm Gladwell, the author of *Outliers*, says it takes roughly ten thousand hours of practice to achieve mastery in a field.

I believe this same concept can be applied when we serve in a place that feels opposite to where we see our dreams being fulfilled. Why? Because this place of service could be the precise place that produces the character that's needed in us. When we allow this process of serving to play out before mastering a situation, selfish ambition and pride are eliminated. The true greatness that follows will influence and change culture, but it comes from a place of servanthood.

DANNY'S STORY

Danny Gokey is a singer and songwriter who was the third-place finalist on the eighth season of *American Idol*. He is a Dove Award–winning and Grammy-nominated artist, and he happens to also be one of our great friends. I asked him to share his story. People may think he was an overnight success, but you'll see that he walked a long road of servanthood and dying to self before becoming a master in his field and before his greatness was revealed to the world.

> I grew up in a large musical family where singing was somewhat expected. My siblings and I sang at church, weddings, family get-togethers, and just about anywhere else we could. Though it was normal for my family to sing, I still needed encouragement that I had talent myself. When I was twelve my father mentioned to my mother that I had a good voice. It was the first time I remember feeling I was good at something.
>
> At nineteen, I was visiting a church to hear a guest preacher. He spoke to me, calling out things I had never before shared with anyone. He told me I would have a

music career and impact thousands. He said I would be a deliverer like Moses. At the time I was a scrawny late bloomer with large glasses and a face full of pimples. And I was short for my age. I did not look the part.

I remember thinking, *God, how are You going to do all that You have spoken to me through this preacher?* Little did I know that it would be just a few months later that I'd walk into another church and encounter God in a way that would change the trajectory of my life.

Faith Builders was a church filled with people who were on fire for God. The music team, young people my age who were passionate about their worship to the Lord, was like nothing I'd ever heard or seen. I became part of the church and joined the worship team. At the time my only desire was to be one of them, but the pastor evidently saw something more in me and asked me to lead the service on my first Sunday. I was so nervous I led the service with my back turned to the crowd. I thought it would surely be my last time in the front, but nope. The pastor continued to ask me to lead every week.

I learned and grew so much in this season, which lasted around eight years. And it was here my own personal career in music began to develop. Interestingly enough, it was also here that the Lord began to deal with my heart. I felt Him ask me to lay down my efforts to pursue a career in music. God impressed upon me that I should pour my gifts and talents into serving the local church rather than serving my own ambitions. And that in doing this, He would fulfill the personal desire I had to actually have a career in music.

It didn't make sense to me. That's not the typical pathway to getting a solo career. It always takes connections, putting yourself out there, and pouring your whole focus into "making it happen." Thankfully, because the idea of having a music career was so new, it was not difficult for me to lay down my efforts and desires and simply obey God.

Over time, though, frustration started barreling in. The feelings of excitement of leading the worship team in the local church had worn off. Serving others felt like a burden and a sacrifice. It was obvious my dream was delayed and not happening the way I thought it should. It felt like I was going in the absolute opposite direction of my supposed destiny.

Serving in the local church taught me an important lesson. I had to die to the way I thought my dream should look and how I felt it should come to pass. Sure, there's always excitement in the beginning, but when the excitement is gone, God searches the heart and tests the strength of the relationship to see if we are trusting Him.

During a season of servanthood, God uses people and situations in our lives to press certain buttons. Servants don't have a right to question their master. They follow orders and obey. In my case, I had to not only work at the two church campuses thirty to forty hours between weeknights and all day on Sunday, but I would also have to have a second job in order to pay the bills that my meager church salary wouldn't cover. There I was, Monday through Friday, working forty to fifty hours a week driving a semi-truck in an attempt to bring in more money. I felt like I was going in the total opposite direction.

I had to do battle within myself for what didn't seem fair or right. What I was reaping was nowhere near the level of what I was sacrificing and sowing. Between the two jobs I worked, and my wife Sophia's job, we were still barely getting by. I wondered how this could be God's will. I had read the scriptures about how God desires to prosper His people and make them great, yet we weren't seeing it. Although we had seen God come through finan-cially in many miraculous ways, I was tired of struggling and worrying about money all the time.

We began to pray that God would make a way for me to get a pay increase at church so I could quit my trucking job. I even had the bright idea of starting my own music ministry outside of the church. Even though it made no logical sense to an outward observer, I felt God tell me it was not yet time and that we were to keep pursuing His plan. He asked me to continue to serve until further notice.

I came home late from church one night with tears in my eyes. After much praying, God had not changed any-thing. I told Sophia, "This has to be the will of God. We must accept that He sees something that we don't." We didn't know then that God was working on me, building me on the inside for something greater that was to come.

Several months into this season, at the age of twenty-seven, I was sitting in my semitruck waiting for it to be unloaded when I came to the conclusion that I had missed God. Don't get me wrong. I wasn't resentful, and my trust in Him was at an all-time high. I just thought that if it really was God's will, I would have made it by now. I decided then and there that if I had to drive a truck and serve in my local church for the rest of my life that I would do it. I wasn't happy about it, but I chose to surrender my dream and lay it down as the cost of serving God.

Little did I know that the biggest blow was yet to come. Sophia had been battling a heart condition her whole life and had been in and out of the hospital throughout our marriage. Nine months after the realization that I must have missed God and messed up my dream in music, Sophia underwent a routine heart surgery and then unexpectedly passed away. This was the blow that finally crushed me.

All the years of trusting God and believing that He would heal my wife, all the time we had spent in ministry, solely focused on building His kingdom, and He had let me down! I had done everything He asked of me, but He hadn't kept His side of the deal.

I thought about the time when Jesus told all His followers that unless they eat His flesh and drink His blood, they could have no part in His kingdom. I could imagine how distraught Peter was in that moment when he saw many disciples turn their back on Jesus. But when Jesus asked His twelve disciples if they were going to leave too, Peter answered, "To whom shall we go? You have the words of eternal life" (John 6:68). Jesus was the only thing Peter had, and that's how I felt as well. Where would I go?

I was disappointed, angry, discouraged, and upset, but I knew I needed God. Even though I had to stand by the casket of my wife and watch them bury her along with the dreams we had shared together, I knew I had no other choice but to trust God. As I placed my trust in Him, and my heart slowly began to heal, I saw that God was good even though the circumstances in my life were not. I knew in the long run that God would not let me down.

After everything was lost and all hope for a future was dead and gone, a new season began to open up. My wife had always said I needed to audition for *American Idol*, but I had been too scared to try out. Now that she was gone, I did it for her.

I ended up as the third-place finalist in the 2008 season, which launched my music career. The seeds of the dreams I had previously laid down suddenly came to life as God sent His heavenly rain to water them. Through all of the delays, denials, and deaths, I had stopped expecting anything to happen with my musical career. Now God was able to use all of that pain for a greater purpose. I can look back now and see how God was tearing away the roots of selfishness and self-ambition in order to prepare me for the plans He had ordained for me in my mother's womb.

That painful process of serving when I didn't feel like it made me stronger, more effective, and more anointed. It made me a better man. During those dark moments I never could have imagined the message I would share, the one He had spent years etching into my heart, or the reach He would give me through the platform of *American Idol.* That season of my life was the most painful but also the most valuable season I ever could have walked through.

Since coming off *American Idol* and starting my career, I have been able to apply these principles in every season, whether it's been up or down:

1. The secret to greatness is to serve.
2. The secret to prosperity is to first give.
3. The secret to your best life is to lay down what you think is the best life and follow God's steps to the most abundant life.

As I've followed God to find my way to what He has called me to do, I have discovered His opposite principle regarding greatness. My purpose and destiny are not found in self-service but in first serving a vision that is greater than my own.

A LIFE OF SERVICE

Danny has been a faithful member of our church since its inception. To this day he continues to serve our community in a capacity that most people would see as being beneath him. Danny is not only one of our worship leaders, he is also part of our parking lot team that ushers people into our parking lot as they arrive at church.

So many visitors to our church are shocked to see Danny Gokey from *American Idol* wearing a yellow parking vest and waving a torch to guide cars into their spots. This is why we love him so much. He understands that wherever he is placed to serve, he is doing it unto Jesus. It's not about building his platform. He is on the road touring most weeks, but when he comes home, you will find him with his family serving others in the house of God.

Serving is not the most glamorous thing to do, but it is a necessary pathway to greatness. All of the godliest and greatest men and women will tell you that they had to learn how to serve and submit against their will. There is a particular character trait built when we have to deny ourselves and take up our cross. When God requires something from us that costs us, we feel it.

Jesus didn't say, "Take up your couch and follow Me." Jesus said, "Whoever wants to be my disciple must deny themselves and take up their cross and follow me" (Matt. 16:24). His goal isn't comfort, but following Him is so worth it in the end. He asks us to take up the constant dying to self so that we can be launched into our destiny and purpose without pride and arrogance. Then, when we do become great, our lives are not about us but about revealing the glory of God. We come to the understanding that serving actually never stops and it is the highest honor to serve others.

Jesus was the greatest servant King of all, and He saw it as the greatest calling to serve. Jesus came to serve, not to be served, and that is why His name is the name above every name. He is the truest Master, having come as the greatest Servant.

JOSEPH THE SON, SLAVE, PRISONER, AND PRIME MINISTER

To continue on this theme of service, let's take a look at the life of Joseph. He learned the art of servanthood in every circumstance. Even when the environment was unfair, he chose to obey.

Joseph was the eleventh son of Jacob and was favored above all his brothers. Genesis 37:3 says, "Now Israel loved Joseph more than any of his other sons, because he had been born to him in his old age; and he made an ornate robe for him."

It's not good to be the teacher's pet in the classroom, and it's not good to be the boss's favorite. And when you are the favorite within a family, it is definitely not a good thing. You automatically have a target on your back the moment you are singled out and favored among others.

Jealousy is a horrible curse that comes straight from the Enemy who is himself consumed with jealousy for God. Jealousy makes you feel as though there is not enough to go around—not enough love, favor, beauty, intelligence, personality, or fill in the blank—for everyone to have even a little.

That's certainly how Joseph's brothers felt. They were jealous of how much affection their father showed to Joseph. Though it's a dangerous emotion, I can understand why they felt this way—Jacob obviously favored Joseph. Because of this, Joseph's brothers hated him and seemingly could not speak a kind word to him or about him. I can't imagine how it must have been for him growing up. However, every morning he got up and put on his coat of many colors that his father had made especially for him, surely aware of how it reminded his brothers how much more their father loved Joseph than he did them (Gen. 37:4).

If I were Joseph, I would have hung that coat up in the closet and only worn it in the privacy of my room. I may have admired it in the mirror, but my desire to keep the peace would have won over. Not Joseph. I think he felt so secure in his father's love that he wore his coat with pride and affection. He not only understood how much his father loved him, he knew he was special from a young age.

When Joseph was only a teenager, God revealed to him in a prophetic dream that he would one day rule over his own family. Instead of keeping it close to his heart to meditate on it, in his excitement he shared it with his brothers. But immediately afterward, Joseph's life went south. Things looked opposite of what his dream had foretold. Instead of ruling nations, he was double-crossed by his brothers and thrown into a ditch to die. I can't even imagine how betrayed Joseph felt. He thought his brothers had his back, only to discover they had been devising a plan to have him killed.

When God gives a dream, no man can kill it. One of Joseph's brothers, Reuben, actually experienced a moment of guilt and went to rescue him. But by then Joseph was gone, having been sold into slavery by his other brothers to merchants who were going to Egypt—far away from his home. Egypt was exactly where God needed Joseph to be because this was the very place where he would one day rule.

Joseph began his time in Egypt as a slave, but then became the head supervisor of the entire estate of Potiphar, a leader in the Egyptian government. We can despise the place we find ourselves in because of someone else's decision, or perhaps even because of our own decisions, but if we trust that God is ordering our steps, we may be in the very place of victory and not yet know it.

Joseph excelled in everything he did. And then Potiphar's wife falsely accused him of assaulting her, and he was thrown into prison. Honestly, by this time I'm sure we all would have been so mad at the unfairness of life and everyone's cruelty that we'd be ready to give up. But not Joseph. Instead of getting mad at God and the waves of injustice, questioning where God was in all of this, Joseph excelled once again. He became the head prisoner in charge of the other prisoners.

While he was in prison, did Joseph rage and wallow in self-pity and isolate himself? No. Actually, he did just the opposite! He continued to serve and lead. Instead of feeling sorry for himself, he used his prophetic gift to interpret other people's dreams, serving others well despite being denied freedom.

When I read Joseph's story, I think of people like Nelson Mandela, who was imprisoned as an innocent man but did not allow himself to grow bitter. Instead, he became a man of honor and integrity, and the world now looks on him as a role model.

I believe it was in this season of denial and delay that Joseph's pride and ambition died and the man who was to be great for the purpose of God was born. At the appointed time, God promoted Joseph and gave him charge over the whole land of Egypt.

THE SALVATION OF MANY LIVES

The more we value each stage of God's process of refinement, even the ones of hardship such as what Joseph endured, the more we will discover that becoming a master requires a season of serving.

In Genesis 50:19–20, we see that Joseph grasped the value of all of his seasons, even the hard ones of injustice and servanthood. When his brothers came to Egypt, hungry and desperate as a result of a famine, they met with Joseph—although they didn't realize at first this was their long-lost brother. What happened when they discovered he was now a great ruler? Joseph said, "Don't be afraid. Am I in the place of God? You intended to harm me, but God intended it for good to accomplish what is now being done, the saving of many lives."

The scripture above should encourage you if you are going through hardship or an unjust season. God is *good* all the time, even when things are going badly. He will bring good out of all difficulties, troubles, hardships, persecution, abuse, suffering, and loss. It may be impossible to see that good while we're going through the struggles, but when we learn to serve with excellence and allow God to promote us, we will be able to look back and see that His plans are better than we could have imagined.

Don't despise the act of servanthood. I truly believe it is the gateway to your destiny of being great and revealing the glory of the Lord to your generation.

CHALLENGE

Are you in a situation right now that looks opposite to the direction you thought God was leading you in? Ask God how you can best serve with excellence wherever He has you now, and allow Him to refine you from the inside out. Repent of any disappointment and choose to serve as unto God. Let go of thinking your season of serving should be over, because a true master will always be a servant.

FIVE STRONG VS. WEAK

Three times I pleaded with the Lord to take it away from me. But he said to me, "My grace is sufficient for you, for my power is made perfect in weakness." Therefore I will boast all the more gladly about my weaknesses, so that Christ's power may rest on me. That is why, for Christ's sake, I delight in weaknesses, in insults, in hardships, in persecutions, in difficulties. For when I am weak, then I am strong.

—2 Corinthians 12:8–10

As I mentioned, I felt the call of God on my life when I was eleven years old. I sensed then that my life would amount to something great. Even though I could not articulate what I would do, I knew it involved something big.

Even when I was broken and lost and at times trying to find my way, the thought remained. I knew God's purpose for me was something incredible. God meant much for me in His kingdom.

Still, in the back of my mind, I was cautious. As I served in churches and traveled, I witnessed many men and women of God who started their race with integrity, passion, and humility, but they didn't seem to be able to sustain that heart posture. When their ministry or name became well known, I perceived a change in their behavior. I watched them become proud of their medals, conceited, and competitive. A person would be one way on the platform, but sadly a very different person behind the closed doors of their green room. It broke my heart and gave me a dose of fear, for better or worse, of the same thing happening to me. I saw it happen so often that I began to believe it happened to everyone. And that was very concerning to me.

When our family embarked on our journey to the United States, I prayed a prayer that went something like this: "Dear Lord, I know that You have called Henry and me to something wonderful. I know that it is all about You, and we are simply stewarding Your message. But, Lord, if You foresee Henry or me becoming in the least proud and conceited, You have full permission to send a thorn in our flesh to prevent that from happening."

I kind of regret praying that prayer. I don't recommend praying it unless you mean it. But seriously, I truly am very thankful for Jesus' beautiful ways of honoring it.

Fast-forward a few years. Our church, The Belonging Co., was going strong, and we were about to launch our first worship record. We were so excited. Henry had not been part of a church album for over nine years, and this was the fulfillment of a dream long in his heart. I remember a pastor saying once that when a movement breaks out, a sound comes alongside it. The Belonging Co. had become a movement, and the sound that followed was stunning.

During launch week, testimonies poured in regarding how the worship was unlocking hearts and causing people to have powerful encounters with Jesus in their cars and living rooms. The sound of heaven was being released, and people were experiencing breakthroughs all around. We were filled with excitement and continued expectation of what God wanted to do.

In the midst of this, one night we went out with friends for dinner. Something felt off, and I sensed they were troubled. When I insisted they share what was bothering them, they admitted that they had heard some things that were quite upsetting.

Apparently some close friends of ours had been questioning our motives in releasing the album. These friends had been highly critical and judgmental of the album, and had shared their thoughts with others in the congregation. Henry and I were floored.

We assured our dinner companions that this was something that often happens when spiritual territory is at stake. The Enemy likes to stir up dissension and gossip; no doubt this was a prime time to do so. We concluded the evening and said our goodbyes, but as Henry and I got into our car to go home, I found myself weeping uncontrollably.

I was surprised at how much their words hurt me. I went through all the emotions that night. I was hurt for my husband because these were supposed to be his friends and peers. I was sad. And then I got angry. I wanted to pick up the phone and yell at our friends, "How dare you attack our integrity?" The more I went over the conversation, the more it poured poison into my heart. By the time I got home, I was furious.

As I took off my makeup that night, I carried on an internal dialogue with the offenders. I yelled at them as if they were in the room and made bold, silly statements intended to hurt them as much as they had just hurt us.

As I got into bed, Henry reached for my hand and said, "Alex, you need to let this go and see it for what it is. The Enemy hates what is taking place at our church, so he wants us distracted over this issue. We have a choice to either engage in the flesh and get angry or to exercise the fruit of the Spirit and love them, forgive them, and show some self-control."

Wow. My husband, the one who should have been hurt the most, since the attack was directed primarily toward him, went immediately in the opposite spirit. He was operating in forgiveness and moving on. "We will continue to love and honor those who hurt us," he told me. "We have an assignment that is much greater than dealing with insecurity and jealousy."

I began to weep again, but this time it was out of repentance. I found myself suddenly overwhelmed by the love of God for those people, and I began to bless them and pray for them. I felt the Lord say to me, *Remember when you prayed about Me giving you a thorn in your flesh to keep you all from being proud and conceited? Well, this is it.* God reminded me of the bigger picture and of the many times He was persecuted and judged for doing what was right. In that moment I was able to take all the bitterness from that poison and hand it back to Jesus. And I was able to forgive our friends with a genuine heart. God took my pain and brought beauty from it. He gave me strength in my weakness.

The other beautiful thing about this story is that the album went to number one in three countries and stayed there for a week. Even more important, people all over the world began to tell us what God was doing in their lives through the worship. We were overwhelmed.

We will all face times of feeling worn down from the issues of life, but instead of letting those issues disrupt us on the inside and cause us to become weary, we have a choice. We can either fall apart or allow God to become the strength in our weakness. We become strong and overcome the Enemy by doing the opposite of what we feel. Living the opposite life injects us with a supernatural confidence and strength that helps us shine a light in the darkest of places and push through the seemingly impossible.

MOVING IN THE OPPOSITE SPIRIT IS SPIRITUAL WARFARE

Need strength in your weakness? Then act in the opposite spirit. Acting in the opposite spirit is one of the most powerful weapons we can wield during spiritual warfare. It displaces strongholds that are warring in the spiritual realm over our lives. When you sense something isn't right, but you can't put your finger on what is wrong, it is likely related to the war going on in the spirit realm. Scripture says, "For our struggle is not against flesh and blood, but against the rulers, against the authorities, against the powers of this dark world and against the spiritual forces of evil in the heavenly realms" (Eph. 6:12). We do not fight as the world fights: people against people. Instead, as followers of Christ, we fight principalities and powers in the spiritual realm. We fight as daughters and sons of God against the powers of darkness. We fight spiritual battles we cannot see with the naked eye, though we can sense them in our spirit.

You cannot fight a spiritual battle with physical weapons. And you cannot fight spiritual attacks with the world's ways or the ways of your flesh either. The way to disarm spiritual attack is through prayer, petition to God, and the full armor of God (Eph. 6:10–18).

For example, if you have ever been yelled at, you know that yelling back does not make anything better. In fact, it makes things worse. Moving in the opposite spirit through kindness disarms hostility and catches the offender off guard. Moving in the opposite spirit wins the battle against the Enemy. I want to add that even if your kindness doesn't change the offender, *you* will change for the better, so it's still a win. You will store up spiritual credits for yourself in heavenly realms that you can draw from over your lifetime.

To summarize, you have two choices when a spiritual attack occurs in your life. You can react in the natural and exacerbate the situation, or you can choose to respond in the opposite spirit to how your flesh feels and watch God move and fight the battle on your behalf. He'll exchange your weakness for strength.

DISARM THE ENEMY

Love disarms those who hate us. Generosity disarms those who steal from us. Kindness disarms those who are mean to us. Encouragement disarms those who are critical of us. An apology disarms those who want to hold an offense against us. Forgiveness disarms those who want revenge against us.

Here's the problem: in the thick of your weaknesses and hard situations, you can't conjure up those actions on a whim. You can't fake kingdom-like responses when your flesh is pulling you the other way. You have to be dependent on God, and you have to engage in a relationship with Him *before* you need Him in those moments of attack.

When we are babies, we are naturally dependent on our parents for everything. But as we mature, we become more independent. As spiritual children, however, it's the opposite. The more we mature and grow in our faith and walk with God, the more childlike and dependent on Him we become. This dependency on His Spirit empowers us to walk in ways opposite to the natural responses of our flesh. When we trust in Him, we activate the fruit of His Spirit: "love, joy, peace, forbearance, kindness, goodness, faithfulness, gentleness and self-control" (Gal. 5:22–23).

At our weakest, God's perfect power is most at work within

us. And it is there that the power of the supernatural gets released into our lives and causes us to live a strengthened and abundant life in Christ.

CHALLENGE

If you are feeling vulnerable and weak right now, ask God to give you strength. What situation or relationship is causing this feeling of weakness for you? As you lean in to the power of His Spirit for strength, what does moving in the opposite spirit look like for you today?

SIX

WIDE VS. NARROW

> "Enter through the narrow gate. For wide is the gate and broad is the road that leads to destruction, and many enter through it. But small is the gate and narrow the road that leads to life, and only a few find it."
>
> —Matthew 7:13–14

I began driving in 1989 when GPS did not exist on cell phones or in cars. Like we all did back then, I had to rely on physical paper maps to get me to a destination. There was no calm navigational voice coming from my phone to tell me where to turn. Just lines, lines, and more lines on a map!

My sense of direction has always been off. Every time I find myself at a fork in the road, my inner compass tells me to go one way, and every time it turns out to be the wrong way. I always feel like I've made the right decision, only to find out after fifteen minutes of driving that I've made a wrong turn. My lack of a sense of direction got to the point where I thought maybe something was wrong with me. Why couldn't I read a map? Why was I the only one of my friends who got lost all the time?

I have been driving now for twenty-nine years, and guess what? If I do not use GPS (which I thank God for every day), my inner compass still takes me in the opposite direction. I cannot naturally find my way *anywhere*.

A compass is an instrument for determining directions. It's a freely rotating needle that indicates magnetic north. My friend, a commercial pilot and one of the most thorough men I know, will tell you that even though he has flown for decades, he would never rely on what feels right. He always looks at the instruments designed to help him take the right course in order to get to his destination. Even if he were feeling great, confident of a course he's taken before, being just one degree off would land him in an entirely different location than planned. The instruments are crucial to making it to the right location.

In the same way, a trustworthy spiritual compass is absolutely necessary when it comes to navigating our feelings and circumstances, and true north is the Word of God. In Psalm 119, the writer meditates on the law, using it as a guide to walk a straight path. He doesn't live by feelings but by God's statutes, laws, and precepts. He says in verses 104–106: "I gain understanding from your precepts; therefore I hate every wrong path. Your word is a lamp for my feet, a light on my path. I have taken an oath and confirmed it, that I will follow your righteous laws."

When we need direction for our lives, we need the Word of the Lord to act as our light. It will guide us and keep us on track. When we decide to go by what *feels* right, rather than trusting the instrument God has given us to live by, we risk getting lost and losing our way.

If I'm at the steering wheel, I definitely can't go with the road I feel is right. My inner compass has failed me too many times over the years. I need to ask myself which way I think is correct, and then actually go in the complete opposite direction.

EAST OR WEST IN THE USA

In 2012, Henry and I took the largest step of faith we'd ever taken. With nothing else but a word from God in our hearts, we moved across the globe to Nashville. At that time, Henry began work freelancing as a studio mix engineer and itinerant worship leader. But honestly, we were walking aimlessly into the future with no direction and no sense of financial security.

I had been wrestling with the concept of the local church because over the years I had seen so much collateral damage. I wondered if the idea of church as a whole was broken, and realized I was struggling with wanting to be part of a local body of believers.

I remember sitting in bed one day with tears rolling down my cheeks and saying to the Lord, *I think the church is broken, and I don't like it. I don't believe this is how You intended it to look.*

I felt the Lord whisper these words to my heart: *Alex, don't hate My church. The church was My idea. Instead of getting mad and disappointed with how many have messed it up, I'm asking you to become the bride I am coming back for. I am asking you to create a place where people belong before they believe. A place where people discover who they are in Christ.*

The challenge of loving God's church once again felt costly. He was asking me to walk the narrow road, and I knew it would only be possible through Him. I knew it wasn't going to be easy. Not being part of a church body that had the potential to hurt me again felt easier. I pleaded with God to allow me to instead be an interior decorator and write books at my leisure.

During this season God challenged me again: *Alex, who are you without the job title? Who are you without the paycheck?* I answered, "I'm Your daughter." And He responded with a tender rebuke: *Then start acting like one.*

And I did. I began to love people. And then seven months later we found ourselves inviting a few friends over for a small Bible study. Within a very short time, much to our surprise, the group grew to over a hundred people who met regularly in our basement every Tuesday night. A year later, Henry and I were still in denial that this was a church. We had resolved in our hearts that we were just stewarding a place for people to worship and encounter the presence of God, so we did not see ourselves as senior pastors of a church.

The following November, a pastor from Atlanta whom we loved and looked up to asked us if we would consider moving to Orange County, California, to serve on the worship and pastoral staff of his campus there. *Is this the reason we moved all the way to the United States?* we wondered. We were financially tight, to say the least, and still had no idea why God had us in America.

Off we went to California—the land flowing with milk and honey, acai bowls, and beaches—to visit the pastor and the church. We were excited. We ministered that weekend. Afterward, when we sat with the pastor to talk, he offered us both jobs. The terms of the positions were more than we had ever dared to dream or imagine. We would be taken care of financially and given solid health benefits. We would be part of a church we admired so much. Was this just too good to be true?

The pastor gave us a week to pray and fast about the decision. We said our goodbyes and made it all the way to the hotel room before we began to literally yell out loud with sounds of joy and relief. We kept going over the terms he'd offered, shaking our heads in disbelief. Never in our lives had we been part of a church that would compensate us in this way. It was like God was giving us a Tiffany box, beautifully packaged with its white ribbon on top, that held a five-carat diamond ring on the inside.

Why was it then that we both had a nagging feeling we didn't want to be the one to share the news with our current community? The more we talked through the opportunity, the more we couldn't help thinking about the people in our basement. Why were we so concerned about their well-being? This was the opportunity of a lifetime. Why should we worry about anyone else?

Soon after returning home, we were listening to a podcast by Kris Vallotton in which he talked about our destiny being wrapped up in the people who are right in front of us. He said sometimes the most obscure and insignificant things are the very things that will lead us to our destiny and calling. He spoke about how we can actually miss our true purpose if we don't discern what God is saying.

I felt convicted.

As we set out to pray that week, Henry and I wrestled like we never had before. I simply could not find peace in taking the job in California. Time was running out, and we knew we had to give the pastor our decision.

We traveled to Dallas that weekend to support a friend who was doing a live recording of her album. Even though we were so excited to be there, we were preoccupied about the decision we had to make. We were present in body, but our minds were definitely elsewhere. We wandered through the day, asking the Lord to give us a clear *no* if a move to California was not His will for our lives.

Before the recording we decided to kill some time at the local shopping center. I looked everywhere for a sign from God while we shopped, even scanning the sales at Nordstrom Rack for the word *no*! Yet nothing appeared.

We went to the recording and enjoyed it thoroughly. There was still no sign of any word from the Lord. We had given Him until midnight to give us a clear sign, and at nine that night, we still had heard nothing. At ten, as the worship recording came to an end, we were both feeling pretty desperate and on the verge of tears.

We were about to leave when a man approached us and said, "I don't know why I am doing this because I have never, ever given a prophetic word to anyone, but I feel the need to say something to you both." Pointing at Henry, he said, "I don't know who you are, but God showed me that you are a worship warrior, and for many years you have been in training to lead an assignment that looks something like leading a team of worshippers. And I just get the word *Nashville* for some reason. I'm not sure where you live, but Nashville just kept coming to mind."

Henry and I were both in tears. It was one of those moments when we knew God had spoken from heaven through a complete stranger who seemed to know the details of our lives. We couldn't believe it; he said Henry would lead a worship movement in Nashville, not California.

As we were wiping tears from our cheeks, we randomly bumped into Christine Caine, a very good friend we had known for many years. She happened to be in Dallas for the same event. As we were catching up, she said, "Guys, what is happening in your basement in Nashville?" We asked what she meant, and she went on to tell us about all the testimonies she was hearing about a "church in Nashville" meeting in our basement and bearing great fruit. She continued, saying, "I've had a word from the Lord that you are supposed to plant a church and reproduce a culture of worshippers like yourselves. You need to sow seed in the ground and begin to produce fruitful disciples, because God is doing a new thing through you. He has called you to pastor this church."

I was ready to pass out! God had given the stranger who had approached us (whose name we later learned to be Michael) and now Christine words for us that confirmed His design over what was happening in our basement. In true fashion, Chris delivered the prophetic message with gusto and then ran off for her car. Rolling down the window, she declared once more at the top of her voice, "You have divine seed that you need to plant in Nashville" before driving off.

We stood there shell-shocked. If anyone was passing by, they might have seen us looking like the proverbial deer in the headlights. What on earth had just happened?

As we lay in bed that night, I asked Henry a question. "If we had a million dollars in the bank, would we even be considering this job in California?" Before I could take a breath, he said, "No!"

We both began to tear up again. We realized we were looking at the pretty Tiffany box with the white ribbon, thinking that what was inside was the road to abundance. Instead, what felt narrow and costly had our abundant destiny living inside of it. We didn't know that fully at the time, but we obeyed the voice of God.

In that moment, we were also reminded of a Scripture passage God had given us when we first arrived in the States. At that time, we had been in Nashville for three months, and I was continually asking God, "Why on earth are we here in Nashville?" God responded one day while I was reading the Bible. As I came to this passage, I felt like the words jumped off the page:

> The people of the city said to Elisha, "Look, our lord, this town is well situated, as you can see, but the water is bad and the land is unproductive."

"Bring me a new bowl," he said, "and put salt in it." So they brought it to him.

Then he went out to the spring and threw the salt into it, saying, "This is what the LORD says: 'I have healed this water. Never again will it cause death or make the land unproductive.'" And the water has remained pure to this day, according to the word Elisha had spoken. (2 Kings 2:19–22)

As I read those words, something resonated in my heart. It felt like God was asking Henry and me to be salt and light to help bring healing to the spiritual climate of this new city we were now living in.

Lying in bed with Henry, I remembered how I felt when God asked us to be the salt that purified the spiritual water of Nashville. It had been a profound moment that I believe gave us purpose in our new city. We decided to follow this word from God as a compass to walk in the direction that God had for us, and we were completely dependent on His leading us through the unknown.

We repented and promised God that we were going to choose the package that didn't look so glamorous. We would trust Him. We would take the narrow road. We would take the road that would most please Him rather than the one we thought would bring us comfort. We would stay in Nashville.

I wish I could tell you that the narrow road produced great fruit a week later, but the truth is, things actually got worse for us financially. The road that kept us in Nashville definitely *felt* narrower. But I have also never seen God miraculously provide for us like He did over that next year. On Thanksgiving of 2013, we went to our basement crew and declared we were officially going to be a church, that we were going to obey the call of God even though we couldn't see the next step, and that we were going to trust God regardless.

California looked right on paper, but it wasn't. I am so glad we chose the narrow road that leads to life, because following the will of God brings the greatest joy. It looked narrow, but it was actually the opposite. It initially felt constricting, but it would become our wide, breathing space. What seemed small and insignificant in the world's eyes opened up the life I always dreamed about. A life rich in purpose and blessing. God doesn't lead us down a narrow path to restrict us. His intention is always to give us His best.

CROSSROADS

The first step to taking the narrow road is walking by faith, not by sight. You must trust God's wisdom to do what is best for you. Proverbs 3:6 says, "In all your ways submit to him, and he will make your paths straight."

Also, when you are at a crossroads and wondering which way to go, don't go by what feels right according to your flesh or what looks the best on the surface. Proverbs 14:12 tells us, "There is a way that appears to be right, but in the end it leads to death."

Let the Word be the lamp unto your feet. Wait for others to confirm His Word. Commit to prayer and fasting, which are crucial for us to hear His voice, so that you can choose the right path that leads to an abundant life.

Last, ask God for wisdom! James 1:5 says, "If any of you lacks wisdom, you should ask God, who gives generously to all." He promises to give it to you. So when you do receive direction, your job is to obey.

The path He directs you on may not look like a road that is easy to travel, but Jesus never promised easy; He promised abundant life. When we choose the narrow path of surrender to our Father, we choose not only what is right but what is everlasting.

CHALLENGE

If you are faced with making a decision between two things and you are being tempted to take the road that looks good and feels better, take a moment and ask God what He wants you to do. Go to His Word. Ask for wisdom. Watch for others to confirm it. Pray and fast. Maybe the narrow road will lead to the greatest opportunity even if it seems insignificant at the time.

SEVEN

FIRST VS. LAST

"Anyone who wants to be first must be the very last, and the servant of all."

—Mark 9:35

Our human nature wants to be the first in everything. Just go to Disneyland when it opens in the morning and watch everyone scurrying to be the first in line at the hottest rides. Go to a Black Friday sale and watch the hustle to get the best bargains. Drive on a highway and try to merge onto the exit lane; no one wants to let you in because they want to be in front of as many cars as possible.

I travel quite a bit, and when I do I love to people watch. It's fascinating to observe human behaviors. For instance, at the airport it's interesting to watch how passengers behave when they are lining up to board a plane. It always astounds me how many people congregate around the priority line. Clearly there is an order for who is allowed to board: all parents with infants, military personnel, and those who take a little extra time due to physical limitations. Then all first-class passengers, platinum customers, and so on. Yet everyone crowds the entry area because they all want to be one of the first to board. The funny thing is that they all have an assigned seat on that plane—unless you're traveling on Southwest. And they will all get to the destination at the same time, no matter who gets on first or last.

I once took a Southwest flight from Nashville and was the last person to board the plane. I mean, the very last person. At first I was annoyed because I'm used to traveling with my preferred airline and having an assigned seat. I've also earned a high enough status that it's a good seat. This day I was traveling without an assigned seat, with no priority, and was dead last to board. I prepared myself for that one remaining middle seat at the very back of the plane.

I waited in line patiently, resolving in my heart that I would be grateful and thank God that I was able to travel on a plane to get to my destination. I thanked Him for my paid airline ticket and for the opportunity to travel and speak and do what I love. My heart was happy, and I was grateful.

I entered the aircraft with a smile on my face. Because I was prepared for the worst, I could not believe my eyes when right in front of me, on the first row, I saw a seat open in between two men.

Some may not consider this a good seat, but to me, it was as if I'd just received a first-class upgrade. I was sitting at the front, so that when we landed I'd be among the first to deplane. I thought to myself, *It's just like Mark 9:35. Those who want to be first will be last and those that are last shall be first!*

Everyone wants to be first. But in God's kingdom, where things are opposite, being first isn't usually best.

Why would God make a big deal out of this? I believe it's because it is related to issues of the heart. God's first and greatest command, seen in Matthew 22:37, is, "Love the Lord your God with all your heart and with all your soul and with all your mind." The second, found in verse 39, is, "Love your neighbor as yourself." The kingdom of God is really about service to God first and foremost, and then service to others.

It's contrary to human nature to serve and love others first, and to position ourselves "last." The only way we can do this is if we love and serve God first. When we make loving Him our priority, we are secure enough to allow others to go before us, knowing there will always be enough for us all in God's kingdom. When our hearts are content to trust God at His Word, we don't need to strive to be first.

THE MEASURE OF KINGDOM SUCCESS

Ambition and success in the Western world can be quite intoxicating. Society measures success by who is at the top of their game. "Making it" means your bank balance is overflowing and

THE OPPOSITE LIFE

your material possessions are in excess. Maybe you're a household name. Maybe you get to enter places first. Maybe you receive VIP treatment. Maybe others around you want to have their picture taken with you. However it looks, ambition has propelled you into a measure of success as defined by the world, and you've reached first place.

Yet how many people in these positions find that their family life is in absolute chaos and the people around them have been caught in the wake of their selfish decisions and are now collateral damage? They may have made it to the top, but it's likely been at the expense of others who have been neglected or stepped on.

Jesus turns all of this upside down in His kingdom ways. He said in order to be first, you need to take the back seat and become a servant of all. He demonstrated this to the utmost in His own life: "He made himself nothing by taking the very nature of a servant, being made in human likeness. And being found in appearance as a man, he humbled himself by becoming obedient to death—even death on a cross!" (Phil. 2:7–8).

Jesus came to serve, not be served. His drive and obedience were directed at elevating His Father, not Himself. And what was the result of His servanthood and submission? "Therefore God exalted him to the highest place and gave him the name that is above every name, that at the name of Jesus every knee should bow, in heaven and on earth and under the earth, and every tongue acknowledge that Jesus Christ is Lord, to the glory of God the Father" (vv. 9–11).

Yes! In the kingdom of heaven we can only go high by going low. My name holds no weight in comparison to Jesus' name, but when I am yielded to Him as a servant, I get to partake in this glorious life, revealing the true nature of Jesus Christ here on earth.

Keep in mind, it's not that Jesus doesn't want us to be great. John 15:8 says, "This is to my Father's glory, that you bear much fruit." He doesn't want our greatness to be about us. He wants us to reflect God's greatness.

Sometimes it takes a process of being humbled to understand that our greatness is about bringing Him glory, rather than bringing glory to ourselves. I am reminded of the story in Matthew 20 where Jesus was approached by the mother of James and John, the "sons of thunder." She asked Jesus if her two sons could sit at His right and left side in His kingdom. In essence, she was asking that they be considered first. Jesus, in all of His wisdom, said to the men, "You don't know what you are asking. . . . Can you drink the cup I am going to drink?" (v. 22).

James and John's mother had no idea that in order to be great and first, her sons needed to understand that Jesus was about to drink from the cup of suffering and death, and that if they were going to follow Him, they would have to suffer and die as well. Her sons' greatness would come at a cost—the cost of Jesus' life and later theirs. Jesus wasn't rebuking this mother for wanting her sons to be great, but He was making sure they understood that in order to be great, they would need to learn how to serve by laying down their lives for others.

We are called to serve Christ—not so that we can become famous, but so that we can reveal the love of Jesus to a world that does not know Him. We are called to serve others, not to be served by others. We need to be like Jesus not just in word, but also in deed. We need to stop and ask ourselves, "Am I representing Jesus well? Am I acting like Jesus would have acted?" Not because we have to, but because we know that to be a follower of Christ means to follow His ways. And that means *all* of His ways, including serving one another in humility.

THE GREATNESS OF THE GREATER CHURCH

We need to be the church that looks like Jesus, talks like Jesus, and walks like Jesus. We live this way because He has wrecked us in the best possible way. He first loved us, so we now freely love others.

Jesus said that in order to be great in the kingdom of God, we need to become like a child (Matt. 18:3). In the Bible, children represent the people of God. In Jesus' day, little children were considered insignificant and often overlooked until they were old enough to become useful. But to Jesus, they were the opposite. The greatest people in His kingdom are not the rich and powerful or the educated. Instead, the greatest people in His kingdom are the poor and helpless, or the least of these. Jesus was saying that if we help those whom others overlook and disregard, then we will be seen as "successful" in the kingdom of heaven.

People who are full of love are better able to position themselves last and represent the church the way Jesus intended. They forgive, serve, go the extra mile, and love their enemy. They choose to be quiet and show restraint instead of shouting their opinions. Their actions speak louder than their words and people take notice. They perform acts of kindness but keep them a secret, not caring to take credit because they understand that God receives the glory from generosity.

Today we have allowed the world's measure of success and notoriety to infiltrate the church. As a result, the world looks at us with confusion, wondering why believers aren't any different from the world. This is the wrestling of humanity on this side of eternity: to let go of the desire to succeed in man's eyes.

It is part of our human nature to want to be the best and first and in control of our own destinies, but when we understand that we are part of a greater kingdom—when we understand God's way of doing things and follow His ways and not ours—He will make us great in ways we could never dream or imagine. The people who follow kingdom principles will change the world. And as the world gets darker, it is easier to shine brighter by doing things the world is not expecting of us—serving one another, humbly accepting the position of last.

CHALLENGE

Ask God to search your heart and see if there is any ambition that needs to be surrendered. Are you striving in places right now to achieve first place outside of God's timing or desire? How should you respond? The process may feel like a setback, but it's a promotion in God's kingdom, where the last will be first.

EIGHT OUTWARD VS. INWARD

"I the LORD search the heart and examine the mind,
to reward each person according to their conduct,
according to what their deeds deserve."

—Jeremiah 17:10

When I was a child, one of my favorite movies was *Willy Wonka & the Chocolate Factory*. I loved getting lost in this world of chocolate (this happens to be my favorite food of choice). But once I became an adult, what struck me was the parallel between the kingdom of heaven and Willy Wonka's chocolate factory. Stick with me; I promise I am not writing heresy!

Willy Wonka wanted to leave his legacy to a child, so he placed five golden tickets into chocolate bars, and the winners would receive a private tour of the factory. Through a series of events, unbeknownst to the children, he would decide to whom he would leave his magical chocolate empire.

Willy Wonka didn't think like the average person. He used fanciful words and creative inventions that made no sense to the natural mind. In one scene, he told the children to lick the wallpaper. When they did, they discovered that each fruit printed on the wall really tasted like fruit!

"Try it," he urged the children. "The strawberries taste like strawberries, and the snozzberries tastes like snozzberries."

"Snozzberries. Who ever heard of a snozzberry?" cried out one of the young girls on the tour.

In response, Willy Wonka turned to look directly into her eyes. And then he said something that has always captivated my heart: "We are the music makers, and we are the dreamers of dreams."

In other words: *Don't you tell me what I cannot do. For I form things out of nothing to become something. My ability to create whatever is in my mind is possible. Therefore, do not bring your small-mindedness into this realm. For you are about to enter into a magical arena of dreams and visions made into a reality.*

Willy Wonka's world was marvelously unique, and four children missed out on inheriting the chocolate empire due to disobedience, irreverence, familiarity, greed, entitlement, pride, and gluttony. But Charlie passed the test. In the end, what moved the heart of Willy Wonka was Charlie's humility.

Charlie was the last child to find the golden ticket. He was the poorest kid out of the five, and the least likely to achieve greatness. He went through the factory with awe and wonder, enjoying every moment. And even though Charlie broke the rules of the contract by tasting the fizzy lifting drinks, which disqualified him from winning the lifetime supply of chocolate, Charlie showed that he had an honorable heart toward Willy Wonka by returning the everlasting gobstopper that was given to all the children as a test. Willy Wonka wanted to see if Charlie would give it to the competition, which would have potentially made his family very rich. Instead, Charlie did what was right and gave it back to Willy Wonka.

When he did, Willy Wonka gently touched the candy and said, "So shines a good deed in a weary world." It was this deed, which was an overflow of Charlie's soft and good heart, that captured Willy Wonka's attention. Honesty, humility, and integrity earned Charlie the inheritance and positioned him as heir to the Willy Wonka empire. His outward behavior wasn't perfect, but his heart was pure. And Willy Wonka took note.

I see so many similarities in this movie to the kingdom of heaven here on earth. God is not looking for perfect, but He is looking for a soft and teachable heart. His kingdom begins from the inside out, transforming the heart and working its way outward through our behavior. As we follow Him and as He does a good work in us, we begin to genuinely look and act differently. The world will notice.

THE DECEPTION OF THE ORNATE

There is a beautiful illustration in Shakespeare's play *The Merchant of Venice* that a lovely girl from my church shared with me. Her interpretation of one of the play's most famous scenes below captures the story so well:

> Bassanio is a young man from Venice who yearns to win the hand of Portia in marriage. Portia is a wealthy heiress from Belmont. She is one of the wealthiest women in the world. Men from across the globe desire to claim her as their bride to get their hands on her fortune. Her father knew this, so before he died, he devised a test that each man who tried for her hand had to pass if he wished to marry her. Portia's father wanted to reveal the heart of the man who would marry his daughter.
>
> Each suitor was faced with three boxes: a gold one, a silver one, and a lead one—each with corresponding clues. Whoever chose the gold box would earn what many men desired. Whoever chose the silver box would earn what many men deserved. And whoever chose the lead box would be required to give and risk all he had.
>
> When Bassanio entered the room where these boxes stood, he read through the clues and responded with this famous line: "So, may the outward shows be least themselves. The world is still deceived with ornament."[1]
>
> Bassanio continued, talking about the fact that the world

---

1 William Shakespeare, *The Merchant of Venice*, Act 3, Scene 3.

is often beguiled by the outward display, whether it be beauty, brawn, or acts that are seemingly good but are coming from a corrupt or vile heart. Facing the gold box, he said, "Yes, gold is a costly thing, it is what many men desire. In fact, King Midas wanted gold so much, he implored the gods to gift him with the ability to turn everything he touched to gold. While this slaked Midas's greed, it nearly killed him because he kept turning his food to gold." So Bassanio rejected it.

Then he considered the silver box. He saw that silver possessed a value, a form of currency. It could purchase a great many things. However, he also noted that silver could also procure unseemly and vile pleasures or goods. Furthermore, he repudiated the juxtaposition of the prize of Portia's hand with the purchase of it. Portia could not be bought at such a paltry price.

Finally, he faced the lead box. The box threatened more than it promised. However, he was moved by the honesty of the lead. It was not trying to be something other than what it was: a common metal. It held no value in the marketplace, but since Portia was the pearl of great price, he must be willing to give everything and all that he was in order to have a true chance of winning her hand and her heart. So he said, "Here choose I. Joy be the consequence!"

Bassanio won his wife. The lead box was the correct one to choose. But he had to really see with his heart rather than with his eyes.

I love how this story shows that it is not what is on the outside that matters; what is inside is of utmost importance. God wants to take our eyes off of obvious and surface things to see deeper into His heart. His ways are always different from the way the world thinks. As Shakespeare so eloquently said, "The world is still deceived with ornament."

We are one of the most materialistic generations to ever live. We are so easily tempted by what looks good on the outside; we are enamored by gold and glitter. But true gold is mined by digging through a whole lot of dirt, and then the unrefined gold has to go through a process before it looks beautiful. We want what looks pretty and easy, rather than going after that which is often obscure and requires work to get there.

God's kingdom doesn't always look like gold and silver when you first glance at it. Jesus did not look like the most beautiful king when He walked the earth. And He didn't entice the disciples with silver and gold when He asked them to come and follow Him. But they discovered that what He did offer was far greater than any earthly treasure—even if it came at a price. And that price was giving up everything, choosing the lead box, so to speak.

Jesus always offers us His best gifts, though at first the package may not seem so beautiful or special. But when we choose the lead box over the gold box, we are sure to discover an eternal treasure, far beyond what we could have ever dreamed or imagined.

The next time you are presented with a situation or a position that perhaps does not look valuable on the outside, be careful not to dismiss it based on appearance. Always look beyond the surface and ask the Holy Spirit if there is a treasure hidden inside.

A MAN AFTER GOD'S HEART

One of Israel's greatest kings had a humble beginning as a shepherd boy. God had given the Israelites the king they asked for according to what they thought they needed. His name was Saul. But King Saul continually disobeyed God because he cared more about pleasing the people than he did about honoring the one true God. Saul had looked like a perfect fit from the outside (1 Sam. 9:2), but because of the true internal aspects of Saul's heart, he failed. His heart didn't fit what was needed to lead the people as a true servant king. As a result of Saul's disobedience, God decided to anoint a new king.

The prophet at the time was a man named Samuel, who was led by God to find a man to replace Saul and be anointed as the next king. God led Samuel to Jesse's house. Jesse was the father of eight sons, and he presented all but the youngest to Samuel. When Samuel met the oldest brother, he thought, "Surely the LORD's anointed is before him." But God said, "Do not look on his appearance or on the height of his stature, because I have rejected him. For the LORD sees not as man sees: man looks on the outward appearance, but the LORD looks on the heart" (1 Sam. 16:6–7 ESV).

Samuel went through all the other brothers, but he knew none of these was God's chosen ruler. He asked, "Are these all the sons you have?" (v. 11). Jesse admitted there was one more, but he said that he was out keeping the sheep. Samuel asked to meet the youngest, and when he did, the Lord told him to "rise and anoint him; this is the one" (v. 12). Samuel anointed David in front of his whole family, and the Spirit of the Lord was upon him from that day forward.

Acts 13:22 tells us that God described David as "a man after my own heart; he will do everything I want him to do." God had chosen a king based on the content of his heart, not his outward appearance. His choice was a perfect fit for the nation of Israel.

Shortly after this, Israel's enemy, the Philistines, gathered together an army and positioned themselves in a battle line to intimidate the Israelites. Among the Philistines was a giant named Goliath, who for forty days took his stand every morning and evening and taunted the soldiers of Israel. Goliath told them that if anyone could defeat him, he and all the Philistines would surrender and serve the Israelites. However, Goliath said that if he killed the challenger, then the Israelites would have to serve the Philistines. When King Saul and the Israelite army heard these words, they were dismayed and very afraid.

During this standoff, Jesse sent young David to bring bread and cheese to the camp to see how his brothers were doing. Can you imagine the scene? David, who has been anointed future king, being asked by his dad to bring lunch to his brothers?

When David reached the camp and heard about Goliath and saw the army cowering in fear, his response showed where his security truly rested. He said, "Who is this uncircumcised Philistine, that he should defy the armies of the living God? . . . Let no man's heart fail because of him. Your servant will go and fight with this Philistine" (1 Sam. 17:26, 32 ESV). David understood the power of covenant: when God is on your side, you become the majority and the victor; you cannot be defeated.

When Saul got word that David wanted to go up against Goliath, he said to him, "You are not able to go against this Philistine to fight with him, for you are but a youth, and he has been a man of war from his youth" (v. 33 ESV). David acknowledged his training wasn't with the army, but he did have experience of another kind:

> Your servant used to keep sheep for his father. And when there came a lion, or a bear, and took a lamb from the flock, I went after him and struck him and delivered it out of his mouth. And if he arose against me, I caught him by his beard and struck him and killed him. Your servant has struck down both lions and bears, and this uncircumcised Philistine shall be like one of them, for he has defied the armies of the living God. . . . The LORD who delivered me from the paw of the lion and from the paw of the bear will deliver me from the hand of this Philistine. (vv. 34–38 ESV)

King Saul agreed to let David fight and even gave him Saul's very own armor. "David put it on, strapped the sword over it, and took a step or two to see what it was like, for he had never worn such things before. 'I can't go in these,' he protested to Saul. 'I'm not used to them.' So David took them off again" (v. 39 NLT).

David did not wear Saul's armor, but instead chose to use his own weapons: a slingshot and a smooth stone. David choose to leave off the armor not because it was too heavy but because it was not what God had designed for him to use. The slingshot he was used to; the armor he was not. He had been training with the slingshot for years. After all, he was a shepherd boy who only knew how to tend sheep.

Perhaps Saul thought David at least needed to look the part of a soldier when he offered his armor. He may have thought he was doing David a favor by giving him outward protection against this enemy. It was what he himself relied on during battle. But that was the problem. Saul relied on what was external—the natural armor. In contrast, David's primary reliance was on God's power. He did not need man-made armor because he was already protected by God's favor. David knew it wasn't the external that would save him. He put his resolute trust in God to deliver him.

God is more interested in what is going on inside your heart than your external behavior. He is not concerned with your religious practice. He wants a heart soft, teachable, and bent toward obeying His voice. Listen to the voice of the Holy Spirit and obey Him, even when it's costly and doesn't make sense outwardly. When you do, you reveal the glory of God.

CHALLENGE

Is there an area of obedience God is calling you to that looks like the lead box? What does obeying God and trusting Him with your heart look like today? Ask Him to show you if there are external things or people in which you have put your trust.

NINE
HATE VS. LOVE

You have heard that it was said, "Love your neighbor and hate your enemy." But I tell you, love your enemies and pray for those who persecute you, that you may be children of your Father in heaven. He causes his sun to rise on the evil and the good, and sends rain on the righteous and the unrighteous. If you love those who love you, what reward will you get? Are not even the tax collectors doing that? And if you greet only your own people, what are you doing more than others? Do not even pagans do that? Be perfect, therefore, as your heavenly Father is perfect.

—Matthew 5:43–48

Henry and I recently watched the movie *Unbroken* together. All I knew of it, and what motivated me to watch it, was that Angelina Jolie produced and directed it, which intrigued me. So I was not prepared for what I was about to see, nor the God encounter I was about to have.

The movie tells the true story of a young American soldier, Louis Zamperini, who is on a search-and-rescue mission during World War II with some fellow soldiers when their damaged plane experiences trouble and they crash into the Pacific Ocean. They are stranded for forty-seven days. Only Louis and one other man survive.

On the forty-seventh day, they are rescued by Japanese sailors and taken as prisoners of war. They are interrogated and severely tortured. When they do not give up any information, they are sent to a prisoner of war camp, where the corporal of the camp develops a particular disdain for Louis.

The corporal singles out Louis, and the torture he is subjected to is so bad and so incredibly unjust that as I watched the movie I felt anger and resentment rising inside my heart. I was infuriated by the treatment he was given and found myself hating this corporal. At one point in the movie, Louis disobeys a command to lie about the United States. As his punishment, the corporal commands all of the soldiers in the camp to punch Louis with all their might. They don't want to hit their friend, but they have no choice.

After two years of constantly torturing the men in the camp, the abhorrent corporal is promoted and leaves for a new assignment. Louis finds relief only for a moment because shortly after the corporal's departure, the camp is bombed. All of the prisoners of war, including Louis, are sent to another camp—the same camp the cruel corporal now commands.

It was almost too much to bear, so I began yelling at the television screen for someone to kill the corporal and be done with it. But the movie continued with scene after scene of Louis being mistreated and persecuted by the evil Japanese corporal.

By this point in the story, Louis and all of the other prisoners are emaciated and weak. Louis is weaker than anyone else, but he is still forced into manual labor. There's a scene where he pauses for a moment to catch his breath, but when the corporal sees him struggling, he yells at Louis, telling him to keep working, and orders that he lift a large beam. He tells the guard next to him to shoot Louis if he drops it.

Louis is about to give up out of exhaustion. The corporal can't wait to see Louis fail so he has an excuse to kill him. But just when it looks like Louis is about to break, he stares the corporal straight in the eyes. He says nothing, but the look he gives the corporal screams, *You may try and break my body, but you will not break my spirit*. And with that triumphant resolve in his internal being, he raises the beam even higher over his head, and the corporal is defeated.

At the end of the war, all of the soldiers, including Louis, are set free. He returns to the United States and eventually marries and has two children. He had made a promise to God when he was stranded out at sea that if He would save him, he would convert to Christianity and devote his life to God, believe in Jesus Christ, and forgive his wartime abusers. He kept his word, and over the years he went back to Japan and met with many of them to offer forgiveness and reconciliation. But the cruel Japanese corporal refused to ever speak with Louis.

Louis lived a long and blessed life. He was not bitter, but instead spent his years sharing the power of forgiveness and what Jesus had done in his life. He died at the age of ninety-seven. He died not only a free man on the outside, but also a free man on the inside, because he loved his enemies instead of hating them.

This real-life story shows that no matter how brutal our abuser might be, we have a choice to love and forgive. It convicted me to the core because I have held unforgiveness toward those who have hurt me far less than what Louis endured. If he could love and forgive his enemies, then so can I.

LOVE YOUR ENEMIES

Is there a limit to loving your enemy? Someone once asked me, "Alex, surely there is a limit to forgiveness for those who continually hurt us? When do we draw the line?" I sat there for a moment and thought about the place in the Bible where Peter asked Jesus a similar question. He asked Jesus how many times must he forgive someone. "Up to seven times?" he asked. And Jesus told Peter that he needed to forgive not seven times, but seventy times seven (Matt. 18:21–22). Basically He was saying there is no limit to our need to forgive. Of course, I believe that you should never stay in any abusive situation, but I also know that the power to heal is often found in forgiving those who trespass against us. We need to put healthy boundaries in our lives, but we also must ask Jesus to help us forgive others, which will release their hold over our lives.

Think of all the horrific things that happened to Jesus and imagine if He limited the number of times He forgave us. What if He limited the number of times He forgave you? What would that number be? I know I have exhausted my limit by now at the age of forty-five.

I told this woman that we just need to keep on forgiving. We can't reduce God's love to how much we think someone deserves our forgiveness. In Matthew 6:15, Jesus even said if we do not forgive others, He will not forgive us.

This command of Jesus was brought afresh into my life recently. I was convicted to the core when I was invited to speak to several women in a county jail. I was so pumped to share the love of Jesus with them over the course of three days. I prayed and inquired of the Lord what He wanted me to share with them so that they could encounter His love.

During this time, I got a glimpse into who they were and was able to connect on a deep level, since I had the opportunity to really engage with women individually. On the second day, I felt Jesus show up in that jail. It was as if He had physically walked into the room. His presence was so strong that every hardened heart was softened. Every façade of hostility was broken down in a way that only Jesus can do. You could feel the weight of His glory lavishing over these women.

I got to hear the stories of why they were there. Let's just say they did indeed do wrong by the law and by people. These were not innocent women sitting in jail for no reason.

One young girl in particular gripped my heart. She was in jail awaiting her sentencing because she had driven a car for her boyfriend while he did a drive-by shooting and killed a young man. She was driving the car and didn't actually shoot the boy, but because the parents of the deceased declared no mercy to either of them, this nineteen-year-old girl was sentenced to twenty-three years in prison. Twenty-three years. It felt so unjust to me that she had to serve that long a sentence when she was only the driver.

A heartbeat of justice began to overwhelm me, and I found myself angry at the judicial system. I felt this was an incredibly harsh sentence for this young girl. As I was driving home, with tears running down my cheeks, praying that God would make a way, I felt God ask me a question. He said: *Alex, I love that you have gone in with such love and passion for these women, but let Me ask you a question. What if you were the mother of the child who was shot? Would you have still gone in and shared the love of Jesus with such passion and generosity as you did? Would you have felt that the sentencing was still unjust, and would you have been able to love your enemy in this situation?*

I stopped for a minute and took a breath, realizing that God was challenging me to see what it meant to love those who are your enemies and to do good to those who hurt you. It put everything into perspective for me.

This is how Jesus loves us. He stepped in as an innocent man and took our sentence so that we can walk free for a crime we were a part of. I lost it and cried a river that day, realizing the power and limitless nature of His love.

JESUS' EXAMPLE

In case you thought perhaps Jesus doesn't understand or can't relate to your pain, you're wrong. Hebrews 2:17–18 speaks to this: "[He was] fully human in every way, in order that he might become a merciful and faithful high priest . . . he himself suffered." He experienced everything we do and felt things the way we do. From the smallest pangs to the grotesque, Jesus experienced hate on every level.

Jesus was wronged when:

- He was ridiculed for being a carpenter's son.
- He was criticized for healing the paralytic man on the Sabbath.
- He taught the truth in love and they wanted to kill Him for it.
- He was betrayed by one of His closest friends.
- He needed friends to have His back, but they denied knowing Him.
- He was mocked and abused by the Roman guards.
- He was abandoned by His followers at a certain point of His ministry.

- He was crucified on a cross even though He was an innocent man.

I can't even imagine what Jesus went through emotionally when all these things happened over and over again—committed by the very people He came to lay down His life for. It seems so unjust and cruel. I imagine if it were us, we would feel justified in holding on to anger and bitterness. We'd believe we had grounds to seek justice. But not so with Jesus.

He never changed His posture toward His enemies. He did the complete opposite and continued to love and serve them. Even when Judas came to betray Him in the garden, Jesus didn't defend Himself or rebuke Judas. Instead, He said, "Do what you came for, friend" (Matt. 26:50). What grabs my heart and causes me to cry is that He finished the sentence with the endearing word *friend*. Judas was right in the middle of demonstrating himself to be an enemy, yet Jesus called him friend.

Jesus asks us to love our enemies, not just our friends. But we cannot love someone who has wronged us without an understanding of true Christianity. Once we have the revelation that Jesus loves *us* this way—that He loved us so much that while we were yet sinners He endured the cross, offering us freedom when we were all guilty as charged—and once we live surrendered to Him, we can give over our rights to hold on to unforgiveness.

There is supernatural power released when we choose to forgive those who have hurt us. I'm not saying you should remain in an abusive situation, but not allowing the love of Jesus to heal your heart and then help you forgive will only keep you in a prison of bitterness and judgment. This is not how we were designed to live, and it is not what Jesus asks us to do.

His power is made perfect in our weakness, and when we feel the weakest in these areas, we can overcome through Him. When the world sees that we can forgive those who hurt us, and we choose to love instead, they will know that we are truly disciples of Jesus (John 13:35).

I believe the world is waiting to see a generation that practices what is being preached from pulpits all over the world. But we can only do this after we have first received a revelation that He loved us and died for us while we were yet sinners. Jesus did not have to sacrifice Himself for us. We were guilty of our transgressions. Yet He stepped in and took our punishment because He loves us. We can never forget this truth or lose sight of it. Only when this revelation is manifested throughout our lives can we truly love our enemies and do good to those who hurt us.

The freedom I have found when I choose to forgive someone in my heart and not just in my head, and then follow through with an action that is opposite to what my flesh dictates, has left me feeling so light and free. It has given me authority over the Enemy because I do not allow evil to fill my heart. I have decided to follow Jesus, and that means I follow His lead on how He does things. His ways are far better than my ways. If He first forgave me, then what right do I have to keep score by not forgiving those who hurt me?

It is time to change the world by moving in the opposite spirit to overcome hate with the power of love.

CHALLENGE

Ask God if there is someone you need to forgive, and then ask Him to help you release that person. Ask Him to help you see them through God's eyes and with God's heart. Then ask the Holy Spirit what it is you specifically may need to do that moves in the opposite spirit toward him or her.

TEN

RECEIVE VS. GIVE

[Remember] the words the Lord Jesus himself said:
"It is more blessed to give than to receive."

—Acts 20:35

As I mentioned, when we moved our family eight thousand miles across the ocean to the other side of the world to follow God's prompting, we sold just about everything we had. And I mean everything. Including our dream home in Melbourne. We arrived in Nashville with a few suitcases and Henry's studio equipment so that he could continue to work as a producer and engineer in the States.

We didn't really have a plan, so we rented a home, and for two years we survived by living off the money from the sale of our house and our life savings. We continued to serve and love on our community, but by 2014, when we needed money for a down payment for a home, we did not have enough in our account.

To be honest, I was upset. Here we were at forty years of age starting from scratch again. Not to mention the whole credit rating system in the United States. We felt like inexperienced teenagers. We began to save what we could toward the down payment, but home ownership seemed like an insurmountable mountain.

One day as I was mopping the floor of our rental home, I threw up my fist at God, resentful that I was cleaning someone else's floor. I had this entitled attitude that I should be mopping *my own* floor. As I began to cry, I felt God whisper to my heart and remind me of the verses in Luke 18:29–30 that say, "Truly I tell you . . . no one who has left home or wife or brothers or sisters or parents or children for the sake of the kingdom of God will fail to receive many times as much in this age, and in the age to come eternal life."

I knew this to be true, but it felt so opposite of where we were at this moment in our lives. I felt sorry for myself; I was doing so much for God, and it seemed as though He was forgetting how much I had given up to serve Him. But my sense of entitlement left when I reminded myself that if Jesus never answered another prayer for the rest of my life, what I have already received from Him was more than I deserve. He paid a price for me I will never be able to repay. His blood paid my ransom for freedom, and I am forever grateful.

I made a choice to be grateful and repented for looking through the eyes of lack. I knew God would fulfill what He had promised according to the scripture in Luke, but it would only happen in the fullness of time (Hab. 2:3). Then I finished mopping the floor with praise and thanksgiving in my heart and went about my day.

It's just a few years later, and God has not only replaced every cent sown into this season of serving Him, He has far exceeded our dreams of owning a beautiful home in Franklin, Tennessee. He miraculously provided for us financially so that we could purchase land at the right time, and even though we had to wait three more years to build on the property, in that time the market went up significantly. The value of the land increased to the exact financial amount we had brought over from Australia. That amount became our full down payment for the building of our new home. Our home is a tangible representation of the reality that we cannot out-give God. He promised in Matthew 6:33 that if we "seek first his kingdom and his righteousness," He will be sure to add everything we need to our lives. We do not need to worry about a thing.

God's economy does not make sense to the natural mind, but kingdom ways prove it is much better to give than receive. If we trust Him in this and follow His way of doing things, we will never be forsaken. And the best part about it is that God gets the glory for the miracles in our lives.

MIA'S STORY

One of my beautiful friends is also one of the most generous people I know. She takes advantage of every opportunity to give to anyone who has a need. She is the first one to pay for a meal, knows just what a person needs at exactly the time they need it, and gives to strangers like they are her best friend. But she was not always like this.

I have witnessed her living in this kingdom way, opposite to the world, and have seen firsthand that the more she gives, the more she receives. As Scripture promises, the glory of God is revealed every time she sows generously into a life. And then her own world gets larger. Here is her story of how she learned the kingdom principle of giving and how it has changed her life for the better.

We didn't have a lot when I was growing up. In fact, most of my friends still don't know that when I was young, I lived in my mum's car for six months. Then we lived in a women's shelter. We often lived on food stamps and got Christmas gifts that were donated by the Salvation Army. It was actually how I came to know Jesus, but that's a story for another day.

I used to think that it would have been easier for me to have a better understanding of generosity and giving if I'd grown up in a different environment or financial situation. I didn't have a dad, and we were always living in such extreme lack. My normal was secondhand, second-rate everything. I often believed that if my experience were different, my outlook would be different.

I think there is a cycle of fear when it comes to finances. When you have nothing, it's easy to believe that things will always be this way; when you have a little, it's easy to be so afraid of never having more that you hold on too tightly to the little that you have. I can relate to both postures.

It's been a long road of obediently saying yes after costly yes for me to change that posture of fear, which is centered around always being in lack, to the posture of knowing God is my provider and therefore I need not fear in this area. My expectations did not change because my circumstances changed. Quite the opposite, in fact. I have had to change my expectations in order to see my circumstances change, and over and over, that is exactly what happened.

It wasn't one big moment or one big sacrifice that shifted things, but instead, a lot of little moments stretched me outside of my comfort zone. Every time I was presented with an opportunity to be generous, I had a choice to be stingy and fearful or generous and full of faith. I was given many opportunities to participate in hidden acts of generosity. It wasn't a class I finally graduated from, but instead, I experienced layers of the same thing that revealed more of who God really is and how His kingdom operates.

I've been given so much advice over the years from well-meaning people on how to be a good steward of my finances so that I can get ahead in life. While much of it has been helpful, nothing has shifted my view of finances more than taking God at His Word and doing things very literally His way. Being a saver and making smart investments don't oppose good stewardship and wisdom, but God's way of stewarding finances just goes further. The Bible says to sow generously and you will reap generously. Luke 6:38 says, "Give, and it will be given to you. A good measure, pressed down, shaken together and running over, will be poured into your lap. For with the measure you use, it will be measured to you."

I remember when I was fifteen years old, I got a paycheck of $63.00 every week, which most people would think was quite small. But I remember learning from a young age to put God first in my finances, and so I gave God $10.00 a week as my tithe. It was more than the 10 percent I was encouraged to give because I was so grateful God had given me this job in the first place. As I learned to give Him my first, I watched how He would always bless me in ways I didn't foresee or expect. Finances and blessings would come from out of nowhere. I could see that God had a part to play as I continued to practice this principle of giving to Him first before anything else.

The more I looked for opportunities to be generous (because I realized it was always an opportunity, not an obligation), the more I started to see that our God gives equally to the person who is a good steward and to the person who has shown that he is not. He gives to the one who labored all day and to the one who labored an hour.

He gives to the greatest need and to the one who already has a surplus. His nature is and always has been kindness, whether we deserve it or not. It's why He is so beautiful. Giving to something that promises a return is an investment, but giving when there's nothing in it for you is the heartbeat of generosity and the kind of giving that yields supernatural results.

There have been so many times when I've given with that kind of understanding, such as giving beyond tithing. That kind of giving has made me look foolish to others. And that's okay. Sometimes the kingdom does look foolish. After all, it is the opposite of what feels natural.

I'm a songwriter. I've been doing it for eighteen years. It's probably one of the most unstable careers in the world. You never know if you're going to get work. You never know if an idea is going to land, and even if it does, you probably won't get paid for it until about two years after its conception. You get paid every six months instead of every week. It's an industry that has been declining financially, and so many live in fear about where their next check is coming from.

But the music industry is also where I've seen generosity defy all of those things. God has consistently surprised me and shown me that He can be trusted and that He still owns the cattle on a thousand hills.

I started with tithing. And then I began to look for ways to be generous beyond that. At first it was paying for someone's coffee when I knew they could afford it more than I could. After a while, it turned into buying groceries for a family or giving someone money toward his or her rent. Then it became flights to allow people to see their families on the other side of the world or paying off people's credit card debt. One day I think it will be giving away houses and who knows what else. All I know is that the world of the generous really does get larger and larger, and that God has shown me again and again that I can never out-give Him. He's always one step ahead, and there's no fear in that.

IT IS BETTER TO GIVE THAN TO RECEIVE

Giving in God's economy is completely opposite of giving and investing in the world's economy. This area of finances is the only area in the Bible that God says to test Him in. And I believe it's because He wants to show you how good He is and how faithful He is to His Word.

Malachi 3:10 says, "'Bring the whole tithe into the storehouse, that there may be food in my house. Test me in this,' says the LORD Almighty, 'and see if I will not throw open the floodgates of heaven and pour out so much blessing that there will not be room enough to store it.'" Wow! This is His promise, and I have seen firsthand that this is true in my life. Henry and I have been faithful to tithe whether we have been in plenty or in want. I have watched God pour out so much blessing that at times it has felt overwhelming to be on the receiving end of His generosity.

God cannot be mocked, and when He decrees a principle, it stands for eternity. One of those principles is that of sowing and reaping: what you sow you will also reap (Gal. 6:7–9). I have witnessed countless stories and testimonies of people who chose to invest in the kingdom of God and were rewarded with more than they could have ever dared to dream of, ask for, or imagine. That is who God is—the God of more than enough.

Of course, it's not the amount that interests God but rather the state of your heart. Consider the story in Luke 21:1–4. These four short verses say so much. Jesus was in the temple courts watching what the people were putting into the temple treasury. Can you believe that? He was *watching*. God is clearly interested in our offerings. On this particular occasion, Jesus saw the rich men putting in their gifts and a poor widow putting in two very small copper coins. "'Truly I tell you,' he said, 'this poor widow has put in more than all the others. All these people gave their gifts out of their wealth; but she out of her poverty put in all she had to live on'" (vv. 3–4).

This story has always fascinated me because it's natural for people to be impressed by the rich giving large amounts, but Jesus was taken by the poor widow. It wasn't the amount she gave; it was the heart with which she gave. She gave her last pennies to the Lord, whereas the rich gave their spare change. Her giving of everything caught the Lord's attention. She put God first, trusting Him with all she had and feeling that she owed it all to Him. This is the opposite of how the world sees things.

We never hear about this woman again and we don't know how her story ends, but I can tell you that whenever I have given everything to God in my own life, He returns it to me, pressed down, shaken together, and running over into my lap.

You can never out-give God. He doesn't want your money; He wants your heart. The Bible tells us in Matthew 6:21 that "where your treasure is, there your heart will be also." I believe that God's treasures are not things, but people. The fact that He gave up His greatest treasure, Jesus, so that He could bring us back to right relationship with Him speaks to this. The Bible says it so beautifully in Romans 8:32: "He who did not spare his own Son, but gave him up for us all—how will he not also, along with him, graciously give us all things?" If God doesn't withhold His best, then we should not withhold our best either.

CHALLENGE

Ask the Lord what it is you need to do today in the area of generosity. Perhaps it's related to giving to your church or altering the amount you tithe. Maybe see if there is someone He wants you to be generous to. Make a note and watch God reward your generosity.

ELEVEN

WISE VS. FOOLISH

> But God chose the foolish things of the world to shame the wise; God chose the weak things of the world to shame the strong. God chose the lowly things of this world and the despised things—and the things that are not—to nullify the things that are, so that no one may boast before him.
>
> —1 Corinthians 1:27–29

It was an average day like every other day. I was twenty-two and working part-time as a secretary for a law firm in my hometown. It was not my dream job, but my father had always told us that if we don't work we don't eat, and that if we worked hard and served diligently, one day we would get the opportunity to work in our dream job.

I had recently completed one year of Bible college and was also volunteering part-time at the church, serving in any capacity I could. Having felt the call as a young girl, I knew that working in the church was part of my destiny, which made working at the law firm seem like a detour. But bills don't always care about your passion and calling, and I was grateful for the opportunity to have a job and earn a wage.

That day at work I received a phone call that changed everything. My youth pastor called and asked if I would like to be part of the staff of my youth group.

I had attended that church since I was a child, and here I was, at just twenty-one, being asked to serve the same youth group that had shaped and developed me and my relationship with God. I was overwhelmed with gratefulness.

After the initial shock and excitement wore off, reality began to set in. I was clearly not qualified for this position. There were so many other young women my age who would be better suited for this job. As I looked at my past, my upbringing, and all the things that seemed to disqualify me, my heart began to sink. The whisper in my mind grew louder and more accusatory: *Who do you think you are? During your time in Bible college you fell into temptation, remember? You had a moment where it all felt like too much and you wanted your old life back. And to add to that, before going to Bible college you had just recently rededicated your life back to God after dating a guy for three years behind your parents' backs. You are not good enough to be called a pastor. You're a fraud, and you should not take this position.*

I wrestled privately with thoughts of inadequacy. Who was I to think I could lead people into freedom when in so many areas I wasn't even completely free myself? Adding to my feelings of inadequacy were my friends who felt they were entitled to the position I had been offered, and rightly so, in my opinion. They had served much longer than I had, and they were a lot more faithful than I had been. None of them had gone astray and lived a double life as I had.

In the following weeks, whenever I walked into a room at church, I could feel the eyes of judgment on me. There was an unspoken question hanging in the air: *How on earth did she get that position?* On the surface, certain people acted as if they were happy for me, but you could cut the tension with a knife.

Some of the other youth leaders actually questioned my pastor's decision outright. In their eyes I was not a wise choice, and they said some not-so-nice things about me behind my back. Even though I tried to believe this was God's calling, the battle continued in my mind. Finally, I realized I had to let go of what other people thought and trust that if God appointed me, He would also anoint me for the task. He would qualify me with His ability by the power of the Holy Spirit.

They were judging me by my foolish actions and discrediting what counted. I knew God looked at the heart. I knew that none of these people had seen what had taken place in my prayer closet at the age of eleven and again at twenty-one. None of them had heard the call of God in my heart when He asked me to serve Him all the days of my life. Maybe I looked like the wrong choice in their eyes, but God sees things differently.

THE MISFITS JESUS CHOSE TO BE WORLD CHANGERS

When our hearts are soft and tethered to Him, God will use even the most foolish of things to shame the wise. This is true for all of us. Somehow God chooses the things or people that seem foolish and make no sense to the natural world to confound the wise. And in this, God gets the glory. His choices aren't foolish; they just aren't made the same way ours are. So what makes sense to God often doesn't make sense to us—in other words, He usually chooses people who are the opposite of man's choice to do great things in His kingdom. He looks for qualities that are often hidden beneath the surface and not seen by man.

Think of it this way. God looks at the whole package. He looks at how we respond to situations when no one is watching. He waits to see whether integrity and loyalty are our first options, or whether lies and deceit are our default. He takes inventory of our prayer life and our heart for worship.

You only need to spend a little time in Scripture to see that God's choices have always been incredibly different from man's. Consider these other examples:

122

- Jacob: A deceiver and supplanter was chosen to become one of the fathers of the nation of Israel.
- David: A small teenager was chosen to slay a mighty giant warrior of battle with only a slingshot and five smooth stones.
- Moses: A man with a stutter was chosen to speak to the king and deliver millions of Jews from slavery.
- Gideon: A fearful one was chosen to lead a small army to unbelievable victory.
- Peter: An unpredictable fisherman was chosen to build God's church.
- Paul: A terrorist and persecutor of Christians was chosen to become the spokesman on grace and to write two-thirds of the New Testament.

During Jesus' time, when rabbis chose disciples, they looked for successors: students of the law who would replicate and represent the rabbi. But this is the complete opposite of what Jesus did when He chose His twelve disciples. They were uneducated, rough misfits. He chose men who seemed foolish in the natural. Jesus chose a tax collector, a zealot, and a bunch of fishermen, as well as others who had no job description at all included in Scripture. Unlikely choices, but this is why I love Jesus. He likes to confound the wise by choosing things they consider foolish. Scripture tells us, "When they saw the courage of Peter and John and realized that they were unschooled, ordinary men, they were astonished and they took note that these men had been with Jesus" (Acts 4:13). Jesus set the stage for people to wonder about the kingdom He was introducing.

When Jesus chose the Twelve by telling them, "Come, follow me" (Mark 1:17), He was essentially operating opposite of the way students came to follow rabbis. The standard practice was for the student to pursue the rabbi, not for the rabbi to call the student. The best students would seek to follow a famous rabbi; however, most students ended up returning to their families and taking up the family trade. Rabbis only permitted the very best to follow them.

As mentioned in the Mishnah, which is the oral tradition of the Jewish faith, the student would replicate the rabbi in every way. The students not only copied the rabbi's teachings, they also mimicked the way the rabbi ate, slept, taught, and more. The rabbi would've wanted the best to emulate him; his very reputation was at stake.

The way Jesus chose and taught His followers was quite different. He approached the disciples, not the other way around. He loved and chose first. Second, His choice indicated that being His disciple no longer required religious knowledge and perfect outward behavior. He set the precedent that we all are welcome to become priests and ministers in the kingdom of God. Unlike the rabbi's need to select the best, in part, to maintain his reputation, Jesus made Himself of no reputation. His identity didn't rest on the performance of His students or disciples.

Jesus' choice to go with the unschooled essentially sent this message: *I believe in you. Though the world may see you as ordinary guys, I see that you will emulate Me the best.* It was a sign of absolute affirmation and confidence before they even carried His yoke of teaching, much less completed an apprenticeship season.

Jesus believed in these men before they belonged to Him. Jesus saw them through His eyes and called out who they were before the disciples even realized who they were. It is easy to see dirt in anyone, but it takes time to dig for gold. I love that Jesus chose twelve men whom society judged as incapable as religious leaders. He saw who they would become in Christ.

GOD LOOKS AT THE HEART

If you feel unqualified or insignificant, then you are a perfect candidate for Jesus to use for a greater purpose. At the end of the day, we are nothing if not for Jesus saving us and changing us from the inside out. We need to stop believing the lies that God cannot use us because of our past or our upbringing, or that He only uses talented or beautiful people. The truth is that when we surrender our will and obey His commands, God will actually help make us more talented than we are and more beautiful than we think as we conform to His pattern, not the world's pattern.

Most of the world is waiting to see if your behavior will change before they decide to take a chance on you. But Jesus seems to rally people around Him who are unqualified, marginalized, broken, and insecure. He knows that behavior changes from the inside out when we are in His presence. He sees potential in what the world sees as foolishness. I think He likes to shock people and reveal His glory through broken vessels. It's time to stop beating yourself up and making excuses about why you can't be who God has called you to be. Be encouraged that if God calls you, He will equip you.

Sometimes we need to look foolish in the eyes of man and not care what other people think. It is when we are okay with this that God can trust us with the things of God. It allows Him to get the glory and keeps us from boasting in our good works. You were set apart and prepared to do good works, so don't be afraid to step into the unknown and show the world who God is through your obedience and trust in Him.

CHALLENGE

Is God asking you to do something that feels way out of your comfort zone and may make you look foolish to others? If so, step out and take a risk. You may never know what the other side of "foolish" obedience looks like. Don't let fear hold you back any longer.

TWELVE

FULL VS. EMPTY

"I will always show you where to go. I'll give you a full life in the emptiest of places—firm muscles, strong bones. You'll be like a well-watered garden, a gurgling spring that never runs dry."

—Isaiah 58:11, THE MESSAGE

Is the glass half full or half empty? This common rhetorical expression is a litmus test used to reveal if a person views life optimistically or pessimistically. Either we see life through a filter of hope and look for the best, or we see it through a filter of lack and assume the worst-case scenario. It's all about perspective.

I used to be the one who always saw the glass as half empty. I focused on what I didn't have and what wasn't happening. This way of looking at things was heightened when I experienced a wilderness season while living in Nashville that first year, because it felt like nothing seemed to be happening. It seemed I was going in the opposite direction of where I thought I would be; I felt as though God had forgotten me. Have you ever felt this way?

We have two choices when we find ourselves in a season of nothingness. We can see this time as negative and empty or positive and full of promise. I tended to see these times with my glass-half-empty mentality, splashing out any water that might have been there. Instead of seeing these times as ones of preparation, I viewed them as places of punishment. It always felt as if God was trying to demote me or put me in time-out so that I could learn a lesson. Whenever the Spirit of God would lead me into the wilderness, I'd resist it kicking and screaming. Sometimes I would be thrust into a desert season by the actions of someone else. Either way, God intended it for my good, and He intends those times for your good as well.

After years of resisting, I have finally learned that if we don't go through the dry desert times when it feels like the glass is half empty, we may never learn the valuable lessons found there. These are lessons intended to strengthen and prepare us for the fruitful season ahead. Though it may feel empty and barren, it holds richness and a full life.

GOD SOMETIMES SENDS US IN THE OPPOSITE DIRECTION

During Jesus' time on earth, He was led into His own wilderness season, which seems so opposite to where He should have been going. John had just baptized Him when heaven opened and God announced, "This is my Son, whom I love; with him I am well pleased" (Matt. 3:17). This was His commissioning into full-time ministry, a declaration on earth. I wish I had been there that day to encounter God coming upon Jesus, anointing Him for service with the power of the Holy Spirit.

Yet, in the very next verse, things take a strange turn: "Then Jesus was led by the Spirit into the wilderness to be tempted by the devil" (4:1).

What? Can we read that again? Jesus was led into the wilderness by the Spirit to be tempted by the devil?

That sounds absurd. He was just anointed, and then He went into what seems like nothing from a ministry calling. In reality, Jesus was actually establishing the fullness of His authority in the emptiest of places. And the "empty" is actually overflowing with purpose for Him.

So many of us may have received a prophetic word or know in our heart that God has called us to greatness. Yet we think that when we are in the wilderness, it must be because the Enemy is attacking us. Sometimes it is the Enemy, but after being in ministry for over twenty years and talking with many ministers who have been walking with God at length, I can tell you this with confidence:

God will most often commission us and then lead us directly into a hidden season that becomes our training ground before the real platform is given to us.

We all have dreams that are God-given. But in order for us to fulfill them, He needs to prepare, refine, and mature us so that we are able to carry the weight and responsibility of them.

If it was necessary for Jesus to be led by God into the wilderness, then maybe we can understand how important it is to our journey. It has taken me a long time to realize that it is in my most barren seasons when I have become the most fruitful.

GOD ALWAYS HAS A PURPOSE AND A PLAN

We are usually uncomfortable with something being empty—whether it's our gas tank, our bank account, our social calendar, or our spirit. Even harder is when we feel emptiness while others around us seem to be living a full life.

Believing that God always has a plan for our good and His glory, let's see how the emptiest of places in our lives can actually be blessings in disguise. Using Isaiah 58:11, our chapter's key verse, be encouraged that God's upside-down kingdom actually considers these times as seasons of being full.

"I will always show you where to go."

We can trust that God will lead us and guide us to where He needs us to go when we choose to follow His ways above our own.

His purpose is always to strengthen us and lead us into a life of abundance with Him. If we choose to find the fullness of joy in His presence and follow Him, He will strengthen us and grow us so that we can be a deep well that others may draw from in times of need.

God will never lead us astray, because He says in His Word that He orders the steps of a good man and woman (Ps. 37:23 NKJV). Sometimes those steps lead us into a wilderness season. He doesn't lead us into this space to punish us; on the contrary, He wants to get us away from all the distractions and voices that are keeping us from hearing Him. God is trying to teach us things, and sometimes we need to be alone in order for Him to be able to do that.

In my own life I have found that when I am surrounded by friends and busy with activities, it's easy to neglect God. I am not saying those things are bad for us, but when they become a primary focus and God gets shoved in the corner, we may need a reality check and a reminder of where our focus should be. God is on the mountaintop, but we don't always have eyes to see Him. More often our awareness is heightened in the barren valleys of our walk with Him.

In my wilderness I kicked and screamed and yelled and threw tantrums. I ate Kit-Kat® bars and felt depressed. I didn't trust the nature of God to understand that He was preparing me for the season ahead. I thought God was withholding things from me and that He had basically forgotten about me. I looked at my life in the present and imagined the future, but I'd forgotten that He orders my steps.

As we put our faith and trust in God, He becomes the light

unto our feet and the lamp unto our path. In our humanness we can only see what is right in front of us, but He sees the big picture of the finished puzzle.

God wants the best for us. He will show us where to go if we learn to lean in and listen to the still, small voice of the Holy Spirit. He will not lead us astray and will certainly not forget us. If He knew where to find David while tending the sheep and Moses when he was deep in the wilderness, places that perhaps looked empty compared against the calling on their lives, He knows how to find you and me.

"I'll give you a full life in the emptiest of places."

Here I was thousands of miles away in a foreign country and it felt like I had nothing, but it was right in the middle of nothing where I found my everything. It felt as if God stripped everything away from me during this season. My old friends were gone, my family was far away, my church was gone, my position was gone, and my finances were going. I was left with nothing but the presence of God in my life. I remember praying through many tears in my room one day. I cried out to God, asking Him why He had forsaken me. Why had He led me to the other side of the world to abandon me now? What had I done wrong? Was I being punished?

I actually had it all mixed up. I thought being in a wilderness was punishment, but then God showed me that He was jealous for my heart and wanted to be intimate with me. He wanted to rewire some things in my heart that I had gotten crossed during my prior season. He needed me to surrender my heart again and rely only on

Him. He wanted to know He mattered more to me than a position or title. He wanted me to be in love with the One who ministered to me, not the ministry done in His name.

I finally reached a point when everything was stripped away, but a song remained in my heart. It was the song by Hillsong titled "Cornerstone." The lyrics became a reality to me. A fresh revelation wrecked me as I realized that Jesus is Lord of my whole life and that without Him, I have nothing.

As I sang this song repeatedly, something broke inside me. I wasn't just singing words to a song, I was crying out and making declarations with my heart. I realized for the first time that Jesus is the goal. He is the prize. Nothing else was ever going to satisfy me but my relationship with Jesus Christ. I came to a place of surrender and said to the Lord, *If I never get to do anything for You for the rest of my life, but if I have what I am experiencing now, then I have discovered what it means to truly be complete.*

I have finally found what makes me whole: my intimate relationship with Jesus. It fills every need for validation and every desire to be seen, heard, and understood. He is greater than any title or position or financial wealth. It all came to one thing that day, and it hasn't changed: *Jesus!* I discovered the fullest life in the emptiest place. I still thank God for that discovery because now I hold everything loosely. Nothing much impresses me except the power and presence of Jesus.

"Firm muscles, strong bones."

In this season of wilderness living you will develop muscle strength and perseverance that builds character. The NIV translation of Isaiah 58:11 says God will "strengthen your frame." And we need strengthening. Our internal disposition, and the muscle of our identity, must go through a painful tearing at times in order for that muscle to be built up and made stronger.

Navy SEAL boot camp is not for the fainthearted. It's grueling and intense, and only the best of the best can endure the training—and the training isn't even the real battle. In the same way, if we can't handle the boot camp training of our spiritual lives, then we'll never be ready to face the true Enemy. We need to be trained and ready to fight, not in the natural, but in the supernatural. Your preparation in the wilderness equips you to fight the real Enemy on the battlefield and to have victory over him when he attacks.

This training will make you confront your insecurities, your identity, and all the stuff that needs to be sifted out in order for you to succeed and prosper in your next season. If we try to shortcut the process, we will bring baggage into the next season that will actually hinder our fruitfulness, causing damage to ourselves and those around us.

God wants to take away all the unnecessary clutter from our past experiences, and He calls us to empty ourselves completely so that He can fill us up with His goodness and presence. We are being fashioned into His likeness even in the empty places, and we must decrease as He increases within our lives. It is not always a pleasant process, but the rewards are so worth the grueling training season.

"You'll be like a well-watered garden, a gurgling spring that never runs dry."

Our season of wilderness enables us to be a place of breakthrough for others. We become a fruitful place that provides refreshment. Our growth and maturation enable us to lead others to freedom. We will become a source of living water that never runs dry, even in the driest places.

Again, this is so opposite to what happens in the natural. It's ironic that in the desert wilderness you would flourish and have living water flow out of you. But this is what happens when you are in relationship with Jesus.

When we discover the intimacy we find with God in the wilderness seasons, we can begin to look forward to them. We can be assured that at the end of our wilderness experience we will have learned to be content and have found the fullness of His presence.

My season of what seemed empty was actually a filling. And it wasn't half empty; it was overflowing. God became the most important presence in my life. He needed to strip away every distraction so that my focus was not on what I was doing but on who I was becoming. I had to make a decision that if I had nothing given to me in terms of vocational ministry, I was okay with it being just God and me. When it *was* just God and me alone, a weight lifted off of my shoulders and I finally discovered a peace that surpassed all understanding. I discovered what it truly meant to have a full life in the emptiest place. It was the most liberating feeling.

To know that God is enough is a full life indeed. When we

discover this life, we have nothing to lose. We live from a secure place of rest, full of Him.

CHALLENGE

Ask God to search your heart. If you feel like you are going through a wilderness season, ask Him to show you where He is. Allow Him to speak tenderly to you and write down what God says about you in this season.

THIRTEEN

DOUBT
VS.
BELIEF

Be merciful to those who doubt.

—Jude v. 22

Have you ever doubted God and felt incredibly guilty for it? Have you ever had a moment when you wondered whether Jesus really is who the Bible says He is? Have you ever questioned if what we as Christians believe is true or false? If maybe we've simply bought in to a lie and convinced ourselves that this is the right way? I have!

Over the course of my Christian walk there have been a few pivotal points when I have doubted the reality of God in my life. Because of circumstances not turning out as I'd imagined and prayers not being answered, I've questioned whether God was as faithful as He promises He will be in Scripture.

Sometimes it feels foolish to believe in a God we cannot see, touch, or audibly hear. But that's why faith is so incredible. It is the confidence of things hoped for and the evidence of things we cannot see with our natural eye. Faith is the opposite of what is natural, which is why it is so hard for people to believe.

GOD CAN HANDLE OUR DOUBTS

Did you know that God can handle your doubts? He is not mad at you for asking questions. Sometimes we think it is a lack of faith to question God. We know that without faith, it's impossible to please God, but doubt is not the opposite of faith, nor is it the same as unbelief. According to the Google Dictionary, *doubt* is defined as "a feeling of uncertainty or lack of conviction." Doubt is a state of mind in suspension between faith and unbelief.

Many times people doubt their salvation. They ask the question, "How do I know if I'm really saved?" This doubt tends to manifest when we think we need to do something to be saved instead of looking at what Christ has already done.

By faith we receive the gift of salvation. And "faith comes from hearing the message, and the message is heard through the word about Christ" (Rom. 10:17). But when we are in the hallway of doubt and continue to feed our doubt, we begin to move toward unbelief. This is where the Enemy wants us camped.

When people are in a state of unbelief, they have made the resolute decision that they do not believe. Atheists have decided that there is no God. They have chosen *not* to believe. In contrast, doubt occurs when you aren't sure, when there is still a decision to be made.

God wants to help settle our doubts and confirm that He is who He says He is. And He has given us the Bible so that we can always find a story that gives us the answer we are looking for. That is why it is so important that when we experience doubt, we read the stories of men and women who went before us. It will help our faith as we read about their own rocky roads of doubt that turned into grounded pathways of belief in this God we serve.

THOMAS AND GIDEON WERE DOUBTERS

Let's look at two men in the Bible who doubted God and were not condemned for it by Him. Instead, God was gracious toward them as they walked out their questions.

Thomas

Thomas is known for being the disciple who doubted that Jesus rose from the dead:

> Now Thomas (also known as Didymus), one of the Twelve, was not with the disciples when Jesus came. So the other disciples told him, "We have seen the Lord!"
>
> But he said to them, "Unless I see the nail marks in his hands

and put my finger where the nails were, and put my hand into his side, I will not believe."

A week later his disciples were in the house again, and Thomas was with them. Though the doors were locked, Jesus came and stood among them and said, "Peace be with you!" Then he said to Thomas, "Put your finger here; see my hands. Reach out your hand and put it into my side. Stop doubting and believe."

Thomas said to him, "My Lord and my God!"

Then Jesus told him, "Because you have seen me, you have believed; blessed are those who have not seen and yet have believed." (John 20:24–29)

I love Thomas's story, and I think he gets a bad rap sometimes. His story shows me that Jesus has mercy on those of us who have doubts. Jesus did not dismiss Thomas's doubt; instead, He ministered to him in it.

Thomas lived in the tension of believing and doubting, which could have turned into unbelief. He had a hard time wrapping his head around the thought that Jesus rose from the dead. The disciples told him that they saw the risen Lord, but Thomas said, "Unless I see the nail marks in his hands and put my finger where the nails were, and put my hand into his side, I will not believe" (v. 25).

So many of us have said the same thing, that we won't believe until we have seen. So you can't blame Thomas. Eight days later, Jesus appeared to the disciples, who were gathered in a house. The doors were locked and in He came. He walked right into the space of Thomas's doubt and said, "Peace be with you." Then He focused His attention on Thomas. "Take your finger and examine My hands. Take your hand and stick it in My side. Don't doubt. Believe." I love this because Jesus knew what Thomas had said, but instead of rebuking Thomas, He came and answered the very question Thomas was stumbling over.

Jesus wasn't in the room when Thomas said those things, but God is omniscient. He knows exactly what we do, say, and think, and He knows what we need to hear and when we need to hear it. He is kind and faithful to answer our questions. I often hear testimonies from people who have been struggling to find an answer to their doubt. They come to church, and the Lord answers them with a word from the preacher or a prophetic word from someone in the church. Jesus still wants to settle our doubts. He will offer us the chance to stick our hand in His side and believe.

Gideon

Gideon is known for being a leader who doubted his own ability:

The LORD turned to him and said, "Go in the strength you have and save Israel out of Midian's hand. Am I not sending you?"

"Pardon me, my lord," Gideon replied, "but how can I save Israel? My clan is the weakest in Manasseh, and I am the least in my family."

The LORD answered, "I will be with you, and you will strike down all the Midianites, leaving none alive." (Judges 6:14–16)

Gideon doubted in his own ability when God chose him to fulfill an assignment that seemed impossible. God saw in Gideon what

Gideon had not yet seen in himself. When we are called to do something great in the kingdom of God, we can go one of two ways. We can say, "Me? Oh, no, You picked the wrong person, God. I could never do that." Or we can say, "If You say that I can, then I will obey and trust You."

In this story, Gideon's response was the first one. He doubted himself. He looked only at his humanity and did not consider that God would be with him and that His power would be working on his behalf. He responded to God's call by saying, "'O my Lord, how can I save Israel? Indeed my clan is the weakest in Manasseh, and I am the least in my father's house.' And the LORD said to him, 'Surely, I will be with you, and you shall defeat the Midianites as one man'" (Judges 6:15–16 NKJV).

God will often take us outside of our comfort zones so that He will get the glory. All He is asking us to do is believe He will do what He says. We cannot look at our own humanity; we must fix our eyes on God's power that works through us. We may have doubts in our abilities, but we should never doubt in God's ability.

God is known for showing up in impossible situations and bringing the miraculous. We doubt our potential because we look at our past and see how unqualified we truly are, but if you haven't figured it out by now, I am here to tell you that God qualifies those He calls.

Gideon wanted to be sure he was the man for the job, so he asked God for a confirmation. I love that God didn't rebuke him but answered his need. The funny thing to me is that he asked for a sign three different times. I have been guilty of this myself. As I wrote in a previous chapter, I asked God for five confirmations when it came to marrying Henry. I needed to be sure. I had some doubts, but I'm thankful God was gracious and responded to all five. Here we are, twenty years later, happily married!

CHALLENGE

If you have doubts about God, take a moment to go into your prayer closet and present those doubts to Him. Allow Him to settle those doubts with His truths and write down what you feel God saying. Last, remember Jude verse 22, which says that we are to be merciful to those who doubt. Ask the Lord to reveal any judgment you have held toward those who are struggling with doubt and extend them mercy and grace, just as God has to you.

FOURTEEN

OFFENDED VS. UNOFFENDED

"Blessed is the one who is not offended by me."

—Matthew 11:6 ESV

Offense is one of the greatest divisive strategies of the Enemy. In my twenty-four years of ministry, I have noted that offense is one of the main reasons people leave churches and fall out of relationships. Offense is like cancer; it eats away at the soul and spreads through the church, bringing division and hurt to so many lives. I truly believe there is a fine line between being offended and staying offended that can make or break someone.

I once heard someone say, "Offense is taken, not given." I believe this to be true. The definition for *offense* is "annoyance or resentment brought about by a perceived insult to or disregard for oneself or one's standards or principles." The key word here is *perceived*, for as the saying goes, "perception is reality."

What we perceive to be true becomes our truth. It's the filter through which we view everything. We often take offense when we have perceived that something has been done to us (or not done to us) based on an unspoken expectation that we hold over people. When that expectation is not met, we take offense. I believe if we can overcome this one issue, the world would look very different.

Jesus never got offended, ever! Even during the crucifixion, when the people were shouting to "crucify him!" (Matt. 27:23), He was not offended. Instead, He continued to suffer on our behalf, despite our ungratefulness.

The people watched Jesus die a gruesome death and they mocked Him. It truly is unfathomable to think He remained unoffended. Not only unoffended, but "for the joy set before him" (Heb. 12:2), which was us. His thoughts and expectations were set on the Father and what He could do for us, not how we treated Him.

John 3:16 says, "For God so loved the world that He gave His only begotten Son, that whoever believes in Him should not perish but have everlasting life" (NKJV). God is love, and therefore there was no room in His heart for offense to take root. He knew the state we were in, and He understood that we were incapable of being good because of our sinful nature. He loved us so much that instead of being disappointed when we continued to sin, He was determined to redeem us of our sin.

When God comes into our lives to save us and make us whole, we need to receive the fullness of His love. Then, when we face inevitable disappointment or hurt from others, we aren't wounded and offended.

Imagine a world where the people of God lived unoffended. Imagine a world where people pursued relationship even when they got hurt. Imagine a world where people lived like Jesus, full of God's Spirit, where nothing could affect their love and mission for the people God had called them to serve.

KARA'S STORY

When The Belonging Co. began to grow as a church, we started to see the Enemy whisper lies into people's hearts that they didn't belong or that the church was just like every other group of Christians gathering together. In reality our hearts were for each and every person who made their way into our basement to encounter Jesus. But some had broken filters that needed fixing. One of our wonderful leaders has agreed to share her journey of walking out of offense into freedom.

> Several years ago I found myself in a random basement with a room full of strangers. I had no idea that what I was experiencing in that basement was the birth of a church and a movement. I also had no idea those strangers would be instruments in changing my life.

Before attending The Belonging Co., I spent my whole life in church. My dad was a worship pastor in a Southern Baptist church in a small town. I grew up with an inside look at church life that many don't get to see. I was well acquainted with the good, the bad, and the ugly of church. I also knew *all* about the politics, spiritual manipulation, power struggles, and general human brokenness that happens in some church leadership.

When I walked into The Belonging Co., I was tired, worn out, disillusioned, and dissatisfied with church as I had known it. But for whatever reason, I kept showing up every week to this group. There was something I couldn't put my finger on drawing me back. Now I know it was the Holy Spirit!

Meeting after meeting, God began to unravel the very fabric of what I thought I knew about His bride. He was beginning to rewire my heart for what church was supposed to look like.

If this encounter with God had looked like a more familiar version of the church I came from, I imagine I never would have come back. When I went to church before I stumbled into the Seeleys' basement, it had been to satisfy my conscience and make sure I had ticked off my religious box that week. I loved God. I have walked with Him my whole life. I was pursuing Him with all I had, although I was a broken mess. But I was just over church. I had been there and done that. I had seen the fundamental mess, and I had seen the charismatic mess. I had put myself out there, committed, made myself vulnerable, and ended up hurt and confused and more broken. I was completely satisfied to meet with God on my couch and pursue Him as a lone ranger, only to occasionally drift into a worship service or listen to worship music or a podcast. Before The Belonging Co., to be committed and planted in a church meant risking being taken advantage of, manipulated, or hurt.

Despite all my hurt and frustration with church, I deeply longed for a place where God showed up and the Spirit moved. A safe place of authentic worship and a place to find true freedom. I was sure such a thing didn't exist, especially in Nashville. But God is clever. I honestly don't know why I kept coming back to the basement, but I did. And I encountered Him in ways I never thought possible.

It was uncomfortable and confronting. The messages demanded that I look inside and apply the Word of God instead of just hearing it, having it go in one ear and out the other. It required something from me. But I stayed because there was something in the atmosphere that continued to draw my heart, even though I couldn't articulate it. Over time our little group of people grew to thirty, then ninety, then two hundred plus. It was starting to take the shape of a normal church, though it was in no way typical or normal, and its uniqueness continued to draw me in.

However, every time our church grew in number or each time some structure or process was added that felt like a form of church I had known in my previous season, I noticed an internal struggle building within me. The basement had been a place of healing for me because it didn't *feel* like "regular" church. It felt intimate and spontaneous. It felt like freedom for the first time in my church experience. It didn't follow a formula, but instead was led by the Holy Spirit, which meant each time we gathered it was different. But it always ended with the same result of lives being made whole in the presence of God. It was a move of God like I had never seen before. God did so much inside my heart there during those early days.

But as we grew, everything started feeling more like a regular church in my eyes, which started pushing some internal buttons for me. Suddenly I found myself getting offended by Alex, who was the teaching pastor, and offended about how leadership was beginning to take shape. I became so afraid of being hurt. I grew paranoid of the same pain happening again. I wanted to leave.

I didn't want to be offended. I actually loved and deeply admired Alex. I loved our church. I wanted to serve and be a part of everything we did. But it felt like I had a concrete wall in my heart every time I tried to move past it. Each new change and growth expansion sent me reeling. The more the congregation grew, the more uncomfortable I became. All of this fear and hurt were overtaking me. I wanted to be a part of everything that was happening at The Belonging Co., but my hurt was beginning to isolate me.

This wrestle and inner turmoil finally desperately led me to reach out to Alex and ask if she would meet me for coffee. I knew I had to address it because it wasn't how I wanted to feel. I shared some of what I was struggling with and told her I was getting offended and hurt by things, but I didn't know why. It was right there in that conversation that God touched a part of my heart I hadn't seen. In that moment as we sat talking, He revealed a wound I had closed and locked the door on years ago.

I realized a filter was over my eyes, and I was viewing everything in this new season through the lens of my past hurts. All of this struggle and offense was not coming from Alex or our church. It was coming from pain never healed or addressed. It was pain that had been inflicted by church, more specifically, by a woman in leadership. I had completely forgotten about this incident until the Holy Spirit revealed it.

Apart from Alex, I had only one other strong female leader in my life. And years ago, that female leader inflicted a wound that stung deeply. It was a wound masked in church politics and spiritual manipulation. And it hurt. What happened to me was incredibly unfair and wrong, and I never fully forgave this person. I thought I had forgiven her, but I think I really just buried it. And buried with that wound was a deep distrust and offense against the church and its leadership.

Offense now came up with Alex because she was a female leader in my life much like the one who had hurt me before. Alex was loving, kind, and not afraid to speak truth, but I perceived everything about her leadership and our relationship through the filter of pain. I perceived the church through the filter of distrust.

I spent the majority of my life going to church. I served, but it was with one foot out the door, constantly searching for flaws and potential opportunities to be wounded. I scrutinized every pastor and every word preached. I questioned every motive and meaning. I never really realized what I was doing: I was building my walls against the church brick by brick with every pain-driven response. Until the Holy Spirit pinpointed this wound, I never realized how I allowed it to offend me, to completely shape and taint my view of His bride.

But isn't that how God works in us to bring healing? He gently brought me face-to-face with the part of my life that was broken, even though it hurt for a bit to face the pain. He wanted me to see how He sees it so that I could find healing. I actually needed things to feel like church to face my church wounds.

What I love about God is that His healing is always complete and never complicated. Once I had this crazy revelation of my church wound, I forgave and released the judgment that was in my heart toward the leader who had hurt me. I released my fists held toward God's house. I forgave, repented, and moved on! Instantly, I felt all the weight of this pain released. It was as if I could breathe again. I felt like I had shades lifted off my eyes, and I could see the truth—the truth about Alex, the truth about our church, and the truth about how God loves His bride.

I love that God's plans are always for healing, always for restitution, always for relationship, always for His house and His people. I spent years seeing out of a foggy filter, missing out on what He was doing around me. When we plant in the house of God, we do get the good, the bad, and the ugly sometimes, but that's what shapes us as we lean in to what His ways are. His ways are always higher. Higher than our pain. Higher than our agenda. And higher than our expectations.

What was also so astounding is that when I shared my offenses with Pastor Alex, she didn't judge me for it; instead, she loved me through my pain and took me by the hand and led me through this journey. She didn't get offended about my offense.

This is what the kingdom of God should look like. We will all face a season of being offended about something, but God wants us living unoffended, with His perfect love freeing us from fear of rejection, hurts, and disappointments.

WHEN WE ARE OFFENDED BY GOD

Have you ever been offended by God? I have. Sometimes we can take offense because of our expectations. I know in the past I have expected God to do something because I had been faithful. I'd chosen to take the narrow road in serving Him, but as I walked along the road called sacrifice, I found myself disappointed at God. I was expecting Him to reward me with the things I felt entitled to because of my service to Him.

I didn't realize how immature I was at the time because I didn't understand that when we choose to lay down our life and take up our cross, it might mean never receiving any rewards this side of eternity. Furthermore, it may be that what we thought we were signing up for doesn't end up looking like what we envisioned.

I am sure that John the Baptist was offended at Jesus when he found himself in prison and about to have his head cut off after he had been faithfully declaring the message that the Messiah was here. Perhaps he thought to himself, *I didn't sign up for this.* I can imagine him remembering Jesus' words when He declared that He had come to release the prisoners and set the captives free. But there he was, a prisoner in captivity, and Jesus was not coming to release him!

John even found himself doubting that Jesus was truly who He said He was. John instructed his disciples to go ask Jesus, "Are you the one who is to come, or should we expect someone else?" (Luke 7:20). Can you imagine this moment? At this point John's disciples probably thought John had lost his marbles, but they went and asked Jesus anyway. I absolutely love Jesus' response. Again, Jesus didn't get offended and spit out words of rebuke to John. Instead, He said, "Go back and report to John what you have seen and heard: The blind receive sight, the lame walk, those who have leprosy are cleansed, the deaf hear, the dead are raised, and the good news is proclaimed to the poor" (v. 22).

Jesus reminded John of who He was and what had been taking place. He then proceeded to tell those around Him about how wonderful John was and commended him for what he had done (vv. 24–28). He knew John was weary and afraid, and Jesus didn't get offended but rather saw him through the eyes of compassion.

I get it, John. I, too, have been offended at God taking me where I didn't want to go while I was leading His people. It has felt unfair and unjust at times. There were times when I was disappointed with God for not defending me in the moment. Where was He when I needed Him?

I could feel my heart becoming hardened toward people when I was actually offended at God. Here I was serving Him and counting the cost of being His disciple, all the while feeling like I had drawn the short straw in life.

I had a wrong understanding of Jesus. And the only way I got out of this funk was by spending time with Him. I had to allow Him to speak to the disappointed areas of my heart and remind me that He is good, that His ways are always higher than my ways, and that He is completely trustworthy.

Like the message of love He sent back to John in his prison cell, He always has a way of entering our emotional prisons and loving us in truth. He shows us that He is good even if our circumstances are not so good. The knowledge that eternity awaits us with unthinkable reward far outweighs the reward we may or may not receive on this side of eternity. Besides, there will be a day when we are vindicated, when the beautiful words "Well done, good and faithful servant" (Matt. 25:21) wash over us.

I have had to learn how to repent in my moments of offense toward Jesus. I recall His own sacrifice, where He moved past offense and pursued us in love so that we could receive the fullness of His glory. That's a pretty good exchange in my opinion. Our sin gets redeemed for His glory, and our response should be gratitude and a heart of worship.

JESUS' OPPOSITE RESPONSE

Jesus could have been so offended when Peter denied Him three times while He was being beaten and persecuted. But instead, after His resurrection, He went to the place where Peter was fishing, made him a hot breakfast, and reminded him of his calling. I am overwhelmed with the unconditional love Jesus showed His disciples. Most of us would have cut Peter off and never wanted anything to do with him again, but Jesus did not get offended. He already knew what Peter was going to do and loved him through his mistakes. He did not hold his actions against him.

Jesus' posture of living unoffended was also demonstrated in His interaction with Judas. He washed his feet, loved him, and served him. He allowed him to remain in His inner circle, breaking bread with him. Knowing that the most intimate moments He shared with Judas would be thrown in His face for some coins. Knowing that Judas would betray Him and hand Him over to the Roman guards.

There were no fractures in His heart to receive any offense because His heart was full of love, and perfect love casts out fear.

If we find ourselves being constantly offended, it may be because our expectations have not been met or we feel rejected. But if we keep our focus on our Father in heaven, then we begin to view people as those we can serve rather than those we expect to fill a void within us that only the Father can truly fill.

People *will* disappoint us, but if our love is centered in Christ, we have no right to be offended. I'm not saying it's easy, but it is possible to love beyond our offenses. The rewards that come from living this way are stunning. You will discover a freedom that money can't buy and will gain an authority over the Enemy that is extremely powerful.

CHALLENGE

If you have taken offense at someone, ask God to show you the root of that offense. It may be that you need to forgive someone today or even let go of your anger against God for something you're disappointed about. Repent and release the judgment. Being offended is a choice. Choose to live unoffended, allowing the love of Jesus to fill your heart.

FIFTEEN

REVENGE VS. FORGIVENESS

Do not repay anyone evil for evil. Be careful to do what is right in the eyes of everyone. If it is possible, as far as it depends on you, live at peace with everyone. Do not take revenge, my dear friends, but leave room for God's wrath, for it is written: "It is mine to avenge; I will repay," says the Lord. On the contrary: "If your enemy is hungry, feed him; if he is thirsty, give him something to drink. In doing this, you will heap burning coals on his head." Do not be overcome by evil, but overcome evil with good.

—Romans 12:17–21

Henry and I had just moved into a new home in Melbourne. Holly was two years old, and we were so excited to begin renovating the basement. We had been renting in Melbourne for two years, and Henry had been working out of a temporary studio. Among other things, my husband is a producer and mix engineer. Henry could finally have a permanent studio space that was not a bedroom within a rental house. This would be the studio he had been dreaming about for a very long time. We had drawn up the plans and were ready to get started.

When you buy a home, you rarely get to know who your neighbors are until you move in. Sometimes they're great and sometimes you wish you had surveyed the street to find out who would be living next door to you. We had always loved our neighbors in every other home we had lived in, and we couldn't imagine life being any different this time. But we were wrong.

On the very first day of construction, our neighbor came knocking on our door, demanding to know when the noise of the power tools would be turned off. We didn't really think much of it at the time because we were so excited about our new adventure. On day two of construction, however, she began taking photographs of the people who were parked outside our home. A little weird, but we weren't doing anything wrong, so we brushed it off as her being a little paranoid and kept working. That afternoon we received another knock on the door. It was our neighbor again, asking us when we would be finished with construction. We happily told her that we were not making any structural changes, so it shouldn't take more than a few weeks. So we thought.

A couple of days later, late at night, I found myself answering the door once again to my neighbor. Clearly annoyed, she abruptly asked me to turn off the pool pump as she had a headache. Apparently I had left the pump on later than the time that was allotted by council standards. I apologized profusely and gladly turned off the pump. Our homes were very close to each other, and even though I didn't think the pool pump was that loud, I wanted to keep the peace.

Day after day it seemed we were always doing something that made my neighbor come over and complain, whether it was construction noise or the pool pump or the cars that were on the street. It got to the point where I feared hearing a knock on the door because I was nervous about what the complaint would be.

Fast-forward two months and construction was still in progress. It was the first anniversary of my father's death. Around ten that night, the sadness really hit me and I began to cry. My daughter was asleep and Henry was working, so I had some time to myself to grieve. Around ten thirty, there was an incredibly loud knock on the door, and it startled me. Who would be at our door so late?

I wiped my face, tears still streaming, and tried my best to look presentable before opening the door. When I did, there was my neighbor, complaining about the pool pump I had apparently left on once again. Even though the pump was in my backyard, I honestly couldn't hear it. And even when I did hear it, it sounded more like therapeutic white noise than anything. I wondered how on earth it was giving her a headache.

Standing there with my face puffy and my eyes red, my heart began to pound rapidly. I was so upset at this lady who seemingly only thought of herself. She had no idea what I was going through, and here she was, disturbing my quiet time and complaining about something so minor. I had had enough and I snapped. I yelled back at her something to the effect of, "You know what? I am tired of you coming over here every time you feel you need to get something off your chest. I'm sorry for disturbing you. Now please leave me alone!"

I shut the door, then stormed around the house, fuming and talking to myself in absolute anger and disbelief. How dare she come over while I was grieving to ask me to turn off a pool pump that barely made any sound? In true Alex fashion, I decided I would keep the pool pump running all through the night. *That will show you*, I thought. Revenge is sweet!

I felt so justified, and my flesh felt satisfied for lashing out at this cranky lady who was relentless in her complaints. *Mrs. Nice Alex is no longer living in this residence. War is on, lady! Pool pump is on!*

I should have known she would not respond well. The next day a man showed up at our home with a stop work notice. Coincidence? I don't think so.

He asked for our permit. Permit? What permit? Apparently in the state in which we were living, we needed a permit to begin any construction over $10,000. We had no idea. Oh no! It was an honest slight oversight on our part, as we had been eager to get moving on our studio build. We weren't aware our neighbor's husband was a builder and knew all the rules. I had poked the bear a little too hard, and now *she* was declaring war.

We were told that until this matter was resolved, we were not even allowed to step foot in the basement. If we did, we would be breaching the law, and they would have full authority to pull the entire structure down. Worse, we would have to pay the city council $10,000 cash in fines. Even worse, we were two days away from completion and my husband was right in the thick of producing our church album. He needed to work in the space or risk missing the deadline for the project.

Can you imagine what a disaster this was? I'm not sure I had ever seen my husband so mad in all of the years I had known him. He didn't even speak after the building inspector came. He just grabbed his keys and got in his car and went for a drive. He had always done this whenever he needed to let off steam, but this time he was livid.

When he finally arrived home, I could feel his heartache regarding the whole incident. He was so disappointed that he was being forced to stop just a few days away from completion. He ended up working in a hole-in-the-wall space that was the size of a restroom. No air-conditioning, run down, creepy, and away from home, which meant we hardly saw him as he put in eighteen-hour days to finish.

At the time, I was scheduled to teach around the offering at church. I began to pray and read my Word like the good Christian I am. I asked the Lord to bless my preparation, ready for a download of revelation so that I could share with His people. It would be such a holy moment.

As I was praying and earnestly seeking the Lord, I felt a small voice impress upon my heart. *Alex, please stop what you are doing!* Wait. Why did I think that thought? I proceeded to pray and again

I felt it. *Alex, please stop praying. What you are doing right now is hypocritical.* I felt the Holy Spirit lead me to 1 Peter 3:8–9: "Finally, all of you, be like-minded, be sympathetic, love one another, be compassionate and humble. Do not repay evil with evil or insult with insult. On the contrary, repay evil with blessing, because to this you were called so that you may inherit a blessing."

As I read this passage all I could think about was the way I reacted to my neighbor. The conviction of God came over me and I felt terrible. I didn't feel condemned, just convicted. Here I was, a minister of God about to preach the gospel to our congregation, and yet I had repaid evil with evil. It was not right.

I repented for my behavior and asked the Lord to forgive me for my actions and to help me with this situation. As I sat and meditated on this passage of Scripture, I felt God speak to my heart and ask me to forgive my neighbor and then bless her with flowers and a gift. He specifically said that I was to be generous! He asked me to personally deliver it to her and apologize for my behavior.

In the moment I felt God all over it, but when I went to buy the flowers and the gift, fear set in. I was actually afraid of this woman. I didn't want to go near her, let alone give her a present. Those fears were perfectly logical in the natural, but I knew God's kingdom ways didn't revolve around what our flesh felt like doing. It was about moving toward someone in the opposite spirit to which they have treated you.

I obeyed. I knew I could not claim to be a minister of reconciliation to my church and not be one to my own neighbor.

With this in mind, I went to the florist shop and bought the largest arrangement I could find as well as a lovely gift. Then I headed to her house. She had large gates that surrounded her home that made it feel even more unwelcoming, but I decided to push through the fear. As I made it to the front door, I took a large breath and knocked ever so gently.

Every second I stood there waiting felt like an eternity. Suddenly the door opened and there she was, with a not-so-happy look on her face. I felt so silly standing there with flowers and a gift. I am sure she was trying to figure out what on earth was happening.

I opened my mouth and said, "Hi! I just wanted to introduce myself again and take a moment to apologize for my behavior the other night. It was wrong of me to react that way, and I would love to come in and speak with you for a moment." There was a long pause and then she said, "Well, I need to get my husband."

Argghh! If I wasn't already scared, now I was petrified. She called for her husband, and they ushered me into their living room. I was still holding the flowers and the gift, but I did not retreat. I began to share my heart and tell them we didn't want to be bad neighbors. I honored the fact that they had lived there for a long time and that we were the new kids on the block.

As we began to exchange dialogue, I learned that they thought we were part of a heavy metal band. Hilarious, right? They were fearful that their street was about to be disrupted by partygoers. I reassured them that the music being worked on in the unfinished studio was Christian contemporary music, not heavy metal. They received the gifts I brought, and we got to know each other a little better during that exchange.

When I left her house, I felt like jumping and leaping. My heart was doing somersaults on the inside. It felt so good to bless them rather than seek revenge. To show honor and love rather than continue the war of offense and misunderstanding.

For seven years we lived in that home, and guess what? We became wonderful friends with our neighbors. They looked out for us, and we looked out for them. They became like surrogate grandparents to our children, whose grandparents lived in another state. And peace remained between our two homes, whether the pool pump was on or off!

THE BLESSING OF PEACEMAKERS

It's amazing that when we move in the opposite spirit to how we feel, life becomes peaceful and pleasant. We can facilitate peace as ministers of reconciliation instead of being ministers of destruction. We can facilitate blessing rather than destructive revenge.

The Passion translation says this in Matthew 5:38–42:

Your ancestors have also been taught, "Take an eye in exchange for an eye and a tooth in exchange for a tooth." However, I say to you, don't repay an evil act with another evil act. But whoever insults you by slapping you on the right cheek, turn the other to him as well. If someone is determined to sue you for your coat, give him the shirt off your back as a gift in return. And should people in authority take advantage of you, do more than what they demand. Learn to generously share what you have with those who ask for help, and don't close your heart to the one who comes to borrow from you.

Since Jesus directed their attention to their history, saying, "Your ancestors have also been taught," it seems there was some debate regarding this Old Testament law. This law was strict but fair; the punishment was to be equal to the crime. But the law was being taken advantage of by the Jewish people; they were using it to get revenge and justice for personal offenses. Like most things in history meant to create justice, the law was being twisted.

The cases that Jesus was talking about were not life-threatening issues or crimes, but issues of offense, conflict, and inconvenience. Jesus was instructing His disciples to think and live differently, to follow kingdom principles rather than laws made by man.

Instead of retaliating and seeking revenge, Jesus wanted His disciples to move in the opposite spirit. He wanted them to take a positive action to bring reconciliation instead of retaliation. The law of retaliation is never a final solution because it's cyclical. When one is hurt, the other hurts in return, and the cycle just keeps going.

Blessing and peace break the cycle of revenge and retaliation. The New Testament beatitudes were revolutionary this way. In them, Jesus asked His disciples to be peacemakers, not war makers. And they apply to us as well. He asks us to turn the other cheek, to give our cloak as well as our tunic, and to go the extra mile when being asked to carry a load for someone. Imagine for a moment how the disciples would have heard that.

At the time, when a Roman official asked a Jewish man to carry a load for a mile for no pay, the Jewish man had no choice. It was the law. But imagine if the Jewish man did it with joy, without a grudge, and then offered to take the Roman's load an extra mile. It would not have been what was expected. It would have been the opposite and would likely have stopped the Roman official dead in his tracks, wondering what just happened.

This is the life Jesus calls us to. We each have something powerful on the inside of us: the love of God. And He is calling us to see offenses and inconveniences as opportunities to share that love. Kindness leads people to repentance, and when kindness is given freely and not demanded, it causes people to take notice. Revenge and retaliation can never impact the way love does.

Matthew 5:9 says, "Blessed are the peacemakers, for they will be called children of God." When we move in the opposite spirit and do what is *not* expected of us, we are peacemakers. When we decide to turn the other cheek, we make a decision to make peace, not war. When we decide to let go of that lawsuit, we make a decision to sow peace instead of revenge. When we decide to let go of our offense and lay down our pride, we make a decision to become the better person and show peace instead of holding grudges. When we decide to let go of our possessions and give them to someone else, even when we think the other person doesn't deserve it, and don't expect anything in return, we choose to be most like Jesus. We extend service rather than selfishness and show the world a different response.

Instead of escalating conflict through revenge, we are called to be ministers of reconciliation. In so doing, we, the peacemakers, will be blessed.

A POSTURE OF NO REVENGE

Jesus never asks us to do something He hasn't already done first. He lived out this opposite teaching on a daily basis. At His arrest, Jesus was a peacemaker when He healed the servant's ear that Peter cut off while trying to protect Him. He didn't resist the soldiers, but instead gave Himself up to them. He allowed Himself to be led to trial.

At His trial, Jesus did not choose to justify or defend Himself, but rather He remained silent. When the soldiers mocked Him, slapped His face, pulled His beard, and struck His back with whips, He did not resist them. As Scripture prophesied in Isaiah 50:6: "I offered my back to those who beat me, my cheeks to those who pulled out my beard; I did not hide my face from mocking and spitting."

And then at His crucifixion, Jesus allowed both His cloak and tunic to be taken from Him. As the crowd mocked Him and threw insults at Him, Jesus prayed for His enemies and said, "Father, forgive them, for they do not know what they are doing" (Luke 23:34).

The kingdom of God is not a democracy. When we surrender our lives to Christ, we give up our rights to our ways of revenge and retaliation. Jesus was in complete submission to the Father and didn't have a say in how He handled things. "I don't do anything apart from my Father's instruction," He said (see John 8:28).

Even though it may have seemed like Jesus was defeated in the natural, it was actually the complete opposite. In surrendering His life and dying for us, His name is above every name. And He is *our* peace. He is our blessing. We are able to extend this to others, rather than seek revenge, because He lives inside us. We are ministers of reconciliation.

CHALLENGE

If you find yourself in a situation where you want to take revenge, ask God to help you forgive instead. Then ask what you should do and act quickly in obeying Him. Watch how He will turn the situation around when you do things His way.

SIXTEEN

WORRY VS. WORSHIP

> Rejoice in the Lord always. I will say it again: Rejoice! Let your gentleness be evident to all. The Lord is near. Do not be anxious about anything, but in every situation, by prayer and petition, with thanksgiving, present your requests to God. And the peace of God, which transcends all understanding, will guard your hearts and your minds in Christ Jesus.
>
> —Philippians 4:4–7

I woke up early on a Wednesday morning and went to the bathroom. Something didn't feel right. We had just had a big weekend leading at our church's worship conference, and even though I was tired from being sixteen weeks pregnant, I felt an uneasiness I couldn't put my finger on. My tummy didn't feel good, and as I went to the bathroom, I knew something was very wrong. Fear gripped my heart, and I yelled out to Henry, "Love, I think you need to call the doctor."

I didn't have the nerve to look in the toilet, but I felt something come out that shouldn't have. I had started to bleed, and my heart was racing at a million miles per minute. We talked to the doctor and she recommended we come in to see her later that day, and she told me not to get out of bed until then. I crawled back into bed to wait for our appointment, which felt like an eternity away. Waves of fear and anxiety crashed over me while Henry did his best to reassure me everything was going to be okay. Something inside me kept whispering over and over that this was not going to be a good day.

"Hold on, little buddy. We're going to get help," I said as I rubbed my tummy and tried to speak life over what seemed to be dying inside me.

We finally made our way to the doctor's office, and she began to roll the probe over my belly. With bated breath, we all looked for signs of life on the monitor. She tried every angle but couldn't see anything. She kept reassuring us that the machine was a little old and that she needed to do several ultrasounds to get a good result. She fell silent and then immediately got up and left the room.

What was happening? She returned and directed us to the hospital for a more accurate ultrasound. A tear rolled down my cheek. Henry and I decided not to talk until we received the second ultrasound.

This ultrasound machine was larger and more complex than the one our doctor had used. As they placed the probe on my belly once again, we looked up at this massive high-tech screen, and all we saw was a sack of black with no signs of life inside. No remnant of our little man was visible. No heartbeat, no baby, nothing but a void of black. I couldn't breathe. I wanted to scream and cry and run away all at the same time. I held Henry's hand, and he squeezed it tightly as tears rolled over our cheeks.

"I am sorry, Mr. and Mrs. Seeley, but you have lost the baby."

Lost the baby! How do you lose a baby? How could this be? How could there have been a baby inside me for the past sixteen weeks and now there was nothing? I was in shock and didn't know what to do. My heart sank as I realized I had passed the baby earlier that morning. I buried myself in Henry's chest.

Just several months prior, before I became pregnant, Henry felt the Lord tell him that we were to have a second child and that it would be a son. *Why, God? Why did You tell us we were going to have a son when he was going to be taken from us?*

When Henry originally told me what he had heard from the Lord, I was not convinced God had said anything because He had not said it to me. Having our daughter, Holly, had been a miracle, and we didn't know if we would ever be able to have any more children, so I had actually grown quite comfortable with the idea of an only child. I had to process the thought of starting all over again with a newborn. To be honest, I initially struggled with it a bit as our little family of three had settled into a good rhythm and I was beyond the sleep-deprivation stage.

After allowing me to vent some, Henry asked me to do one thing for him: pray. Well, I might as well have said yes to the pregnancy then and there, because when you get asked to pray, you realize God is probably asking you to do something opposite of what your flesh is feeling in the moment. I yielded my pride and agreed.

I began to pray and fast, specifically asking God to confirm Henry's prayers through a word or a sign. A few weeks later, a pastor friend from a local congregation in Brisbane, Australia, was speaking at our church. I was desperate to hear a word, but the meeting came to an end and . . . nothing.

As we were walking back to the green room, our pastor friend came alongside me and said, "Alex, I have a word for you, but I felt God telling me not to give it to you in public." Here it was—here was the word! He proceeded to tell me that God had spoken to him to tell me that the number of children I am meant to have is up to God and not me. And that we receive the privilege to bring those into our family that God has predestined from eternity. And there *was* another He wanted to bring into our family.

This was a major confirmation, but even as I knew it was the answer to my prayer, I couldn't help but feel scared at the thought of having a second child. How could I love this baby as much as I loved Holly? How was I supposed to juggle a full-time ministry career with two children and a husband who traveled for most of the year? *How, God, how?*

I had no answers, but I knew I had no choice but to surrender my will. I told Henry I was on board with trying to have another child, and he was elated, to say the least. God had promised my husband a son to continue the Seeley line. Henry was the last Seeley of his generation, so having a son would mean the name would carry on for another generation.

Within a few months we were pregnant. We couldn't believe it. God was right! We were having a son. Holly was excited, Henry was ecstatic, and I was full of joy that I did not expect. Wow! Our miracle baby number two. Would he look like Holly? What was he going to be like? I began to imagine life with our son. *Our son!* I liked the sound of that.

And now, lying in that high-tech ultrasound room, I was faced with the cold fact that he would never be with us. As we wept in each other's arms, we wondered how we would weather this storm that had come out of nowhere. We packed up our things and headed home, heartbroken.

Henry was scheduled to lead worship that night at an event an hour away from home for the pastors of our state. As much as I wanted us home together, we both felt like he was still supposed to go and that God had a specific assignment for him in leading worship.

It wasn't that Henry didn't have to process the grief as much as I did. He was wrecked too. He told me later that as he kept imagining that screen and the void that was there, he felt God say in his heart, *Henry, instead of asking why, why don't you fill your why with worship? Even though there is a void in Alex's womb on this side of eternity, your son is now worshipping Me around the throne. Fill your void and your why with worship. Choose to do the opposite of how you feel right now and choose to worship Me in the void.*

Full of heartache at the event, Henry began to sing, tears

running down his face, worshipping. Henry told me later that as he began to sing, choking up with every word, he felt the pain lift and the warmth of the Father's love wash over him.

I think so often we allow ourselves to be dictated by our feelings, doing whatever we feel in the moment and then wondering why we always feel depressed. There is power in choosing to do what your spirit says to do instead of what your flesh wants to do. Every time you choose the leading of the Spirit, a supernatural transaction takes place. At the moment Henry decided to worship rather than worry and remain devastated, doing the opposite of what his flesh wanted, he experienced a breakthrough.

Back at home, my friend Debbie stopped by to deliver a meal. Debbie is one of those women who not only cooks and decorates like Martha Stewart, but is also a spiritual ninja. She has the ability to look right into your heart and discern what is truly going on. As I wept in her arms, she hugged me with all the force she had. I whispered through my tears, "Why? Why did I only have him for sixteen weeks? Why did this end in nothing?" Debbie said something I will never forget: "I don't know why, but maybe your son's assignment was to live for sixteen weeks."

As I lay in bed later that night, Debbie's words continued to ring in my head. While I still didn't understand, I was able to release my son, Benjamin Judah, back to the Lord.

When Henry chose to lead those men and women in worship even though he didn't feel like it, it was a sight to behold. All the church leaders came together with one heart and one mind and began to worship with such passion and zeal. Henry had a moment when he felt as if they were all worshipping around the throne with Benjamin Judah that night, along with all of heaven. It brought such a spirit of unity among the leaders of churches that were once tentative to join together. It was like his little life brought everyone together for a time that will be remembered as a significant moment.

I'm not saying God caused the miscarriage to do the spiritual work we experienced, but because Henry chose to worship God in adversity rather than getting mad at Him, God turned our loss into something beautiful. Death is not final, and it was not going to have the victory. Eternity is forever, and we will be with Benjamin Judah forever.

And because God is always good, and always redeems, we knew He would use our sadness for something good. Little did we know that just eleven months later, we would give birth to our beautiful son Taylor Henry Seeley.

The word God spoke to Henry did come to pass. Now I not only have one son but two; it was actually a few months after my miscarriage that I became pregnant with my son Taylor, and I cannot wait for the day when we will see Benjamin again. For now, we have the privilege of raising our children, Holly and Taylor, on this side of eternity.

CHOOSE TO WORSHIP INSTEAD OF ASKING WHY

Jesus tells us in Matthew 6:31–34:

> Do not worry, saying, "What shall we eat?" or "What shall we drink?" or "What shall we wear?" For the pagans run after all

these things, and your heavenly Father knows that you need them. But seek first his kingdom and his righteousness, and all these things will be given to you as well. Therefore do not worry about tomorrow, for tomorrow will worry about itself. Each day has enough trouble of its own.

I have stopped asking why and have replaced it with worship. Worrying can't change the situation, but worship and prayer can. Worry leads to anxiousness and makes your situation bigger than it actually is. But when we worship, we remember that God is bigger than the problems we face. No matter how insurmountable our challenges feel, God is way bigger and more powerful and will fight on our behalf. The more we worry, the less we trust God. The more we trust God, the less we worry.

Philippians 4:6–7 says, "Do not be anxious about anything, but in every situation, by prayer and petition, with thanksgiving, present your requests to God. And the peace of God, which transcends all understanding, will guard your hearts and your minds in Christ Jesus." This is an incredible statement in which Paul is commanding us not to be anxious. How on earth can we do that? You just need to read two-thirds of the New Testament to discover that Paul did not have an easy life and had every reason to be anxious. He was shipwrecked, flogged, imprisoned, and persecuted on a regular basis. Sometimes he lived in plenty, but there were many times he lived in lack. He overcame worry and anxiety by bringing every situation to God in prayer and petition—and this is key—*with thanksgiving.*

Did you know that it is very difficult to be anxious and grateful at the same time? Try it. Take a moment and begin to thank God for every little thing He has done for you in the last year. Thank Him for your salvation. Thank Him for your provision. Thank Him for your family. Thank Him for having a roof over your head. Thank Him for the clothes on your back. Thank Him for the latte you may be drinking right now. And as you do this, watch the worry and anxiety begin to dissolve. Allow the peace of God to guard your heart and mind in Christ Jesus.

When we choose to live according to biblical kingdom principles, we will see a change in our circumstances and, more important, a change inside of us. Philippians 4:8 goes on to say that we are to think about things that are pure, lovely, admirable, excellent, and praise-worthy, because when we think about these things, our perceptions of our circumstances change.

It seems so simple, right? So why is it we worry more than we worship? If followers of Christ really and truly took God at His Word and believed in His nature, we never would worry. He works all things together for our good. Even if the situation looks dire, God is always working behind the scenes to bring out the best outcome. And sometimes the best outcome is who we become on the other side of a trial.

Adversity and suffering either bring out the best or the worst in us. I can assure you that as you worship through your trials, the atmosphere over your life will be strengthened. I often tell our church that worry is like incense that goes up to the Enemy and that he loves that particular fragrance. But when we choose to worship instead of worry, the scent becomes repulsive, as if the incense has become kryptonite. The Enemy shrinks back and has no power. Let us not give the Enemy any more power than he thinks he has. We have the victory when we choose to worship and not worry.

CHALLENGE

Instead of asking God the question "why" right now, fill the *why* with worship. Once you've allowed worship to fill your heart, quiet your mind and listen to what God has to say. Lay down your worry and concerns and live in peace today. Watch God bless your life.

SEVENTEEN

REAP VS. SOW

The point is this: whoever sows sparingly will also reap
sparingly, and whoever sows bountifully will also reap
bountifully.

—2 Corinthians 9:6 ESV

A few years ago, while we were still living in Melbourne, Henry
walked through one of the toughest seasons of his life. It was a
time that rocked him to the core, but it was also a time when he
learned more about God—and about himself—than ever before.
Specifically, Henry learned a valuable lesson about the nature of
God and how He helps us reap more than we could ever dream of

or imagine when we sow faith instead of trying to generate a harvest through our own efforts.

I've asked Henry to share his story here. I pray it helps you understand that when unjust situations come against you and leave you in lack, God has a strategy to turn what feels devastating in the natural world into your greatest miracle.

HENRY'S STORY

Back in 2008, I began to sense that God was leading me toward a new direction in my ministry. Doors were closing all around me, and even the most straightforward scenarios began to feel painstakingly frustrating for no obvious reason. I prayed about the situation, of course. And the more I prayed, the clearer it became that God was bringing that season of my ministry to a close.

The problem was that I wasn't *ready* for what God was doing. Things had been going well at our church, and in our worship ministry specifically. I didn't want that season to end.

To give a little history, I'd started serving that church as a volunteer in the student ministry when I was sixteen years old. I worked hard, and I was eventually taken on as a staff member. For almost fifteen years I served the pastors and our congregation faithfully. I even had the privilege of helping birth a student conference and worship movement that are still having an impact around the world today.

When God began closing the door and leading me somewhere new, our ministry was finally on the cusp of achieving that worldwide impact. I had invested fifteen years of my creativity and labor, and it was all about to pay off. I'd already been fortunate enough to travel extensively with our worship team, and I'd produced over twenty worship records—but I knew that was just the start. A greater level of success was right around the corner. So making the decision to leave before we achieved that success was difficult.

That wasn't the hardest part, though. Deep down in my gut, the hardest part was knowing that others would receive the benefits of my efforts.

That hurt.

As I continued to wrestle with the clash between my goals and God's plan, I was plagued by one critical question: "What next?" If I moved on from our church, what would I be moving to?

I was sitting on a plane flying from Melbourne, Australia, to Los Angeles when I got the answer. God began to speak to me with a degree of clarity and specificity I had only experienced a few times before. As I listened, God unpacked for me what was ahead—new opportunities to produce music, new chances to lead worship in new places, and a new path to experiencing God's provision in my life.

Through it all, I can remember one glaring realization: in order for me to step into the next season of ministry, I would need a tremendous amount of faith. The whole idea scared me to the core!

As Christians, we often talk about "having faith," which is inherently fundamental to our walk with God. In its most elemental form, faith is a prerequisite to our belief system as followers of Christ—it is the very essence of our relationship with God because every person who has a relationship with God at any level must display at least *some* amount of faith. In fact, the Bible says it not only takes faith to believe in God, but without faith it is *impossible* to please God (Heb. 11:6)!

Throughout my walk with Christ, I've learned that there are different levels of faith in the Christian life. The first is what I call "relational faith" or "faith for salvation." This is more than just "believing in God." It's the process of actually walking in God's redemptive plan for our lives.

The next level of faith is where God calls us to *trust* Him with our lives, our futures, our hopes, and our dreams. This is the level where things can get a little scary! Like Peter when Jesus called him out of the boat to walk on the water, there is an aspect of our trust in God that can only be revealed when we take a "leap of faith" and choose to believe Him in ways we never had the courage to do before.

On that plane flying toward Los Angeles, I knew God was asking me to take that kind of leap. After a few months of walking through the decision with our pastors,

I resigned from the church staff and trusted God to open the doors for this new future as an independent professional in the music business.

Within weeks, almost my entire year was filled with albums to produce, opportunities to lead worship, and all manner of things in between. By the end of the year, I looked over our books and realized I'd had my most financially prosperous year *ever*! Alex and I celebrated with a sigh of relief as we began to understand what this decision to "sow faith" had unleashed in our lives.

And it was only the beginning! I remember the excitement I felt when I realized that my first year was just the start—that the next year could be even better.

Then came the real break. For the first time I had the opportunity to work with a band signed to a major recording label based in the United States. This was big! Our family was still living in Melbourne at the time, so I knew accepting that opportunity would mean considerable amounts of travel. But I was ready for whatever God brought my way.

I should have known it then, but God wasn't done teaching me about the importance of sowing faith rather than focusing on the harvest. He had more lessons prepared for me.

As the year progressed, I spent about three months working with this band in the States, traveling back and forth several times during the year. I was excited about the project and believed in the band's mission. Still, as I got close to wrapping the final mixes on the album, I was anxious to finally get paid. The record label had paid a small percentage of my fee up front, but all that money barely covered my flights. I had been managing all the other expenses myself, which meant money was a little tight for our family.

Around that time, our daughter was entering her last term of the school year at a private Christian school. The school administrators were kind enough to allow us to split our payments throughout the year because of our unique financial situation, but our daughter's final term fees were now due. In fact, they were overdue. But I knew that as soon as the record was done, I would have the money to pay the school. Everything would be okay.

Then one morning I received a text from a friend asking if I'd heard the news that the band I had been working with had been dropped suddenly by their label. I hadn't. I reached out to my people to get some clarity on the situation. Long story short, the label was in some financial trouble and made a sudden decision to let go of a large portion of their developing artists.

I was somewhat concerned, because the contract I had to produce the album was through the label, and if the label dropped the band's agreement, then the band was under no obligation to pay the debt. But because the band I was working with was a part of a thriving church, I was certain the church would want to get the project over the line and step in to pay the costs of finishing the album and the debt.

"Everything will be okay," I told myself again.

I was wrong.

Later that day I received a phone call from the pastor of the church connected with the band. He told me in no uncertain terms that "sometimes you just have to take one for the team." I sat there in disbelief! I *knew* the church had the money to cover the debt, but they made it very clear that not only were they not going to pay me, but they also expected me to finish the album—at *my* expense! As it stood, between what had already been spent and what was owed to me, I was now almost $50,000 in the red.

After the call I paced up and down my studio, trying to figure out what to do. I felt sick to my stomach as the reality began to sink in. Not only was I in debt, I now had no money to pay anything for our family—bills, school fees, groceries, the car payment. I felt myself spiraling toward a dark place as I tried to battle the rage rising up inside me. I was angry at the label, yes, and angry with the people involved. But I was more angry with God.

"How could You do this to me?" I cried out in prayer. "You were the one that *told* me to leave my job at the church and to step out like this—and now here I am stuck in an *impossible* situation with no way out!"

That night we had a gathering for business leaders at our church. I'd never been to one of those gatherings, but I knew I had to go. In fact, even if it was a ladies-only meeting that night, I still would have gone—I needed to get myself in and around the church community, even though it was the last place I felt like being. To be honest, I don't remember a word that was said from the stage that night. But I do remember clearly the voice of the Holy Spirit speaking to me.

He said, *Henry, you have two choices. You can fight hard in your own strength and maybe have a shot at getting back what has been taken from you. That will be the limit you'll live under—the stress and anxiety of trying to resolve the situation in the flesh. Or you can choose to sow your lost money in faith and allow it to be a seed for the next season of financial prosperity in your life.*

Have you ever had a moment where you *knew* God was speaking to you, but you were also wondering why He sounded like He'd absolutely *lost His mind*? I walked out of that meeting, got in my car, and asked Him, *What are You talking about?*

I became enraged all over again at the idea of not fighting to get the money back—not to mention *voluntarily allowing* the guilty parties to be off the hook. I thought about the practical ramifications of that decision: not being able to pay my mortgage, buy groceries, pay my daughter's school fees. . . . Right there in that moment, I realized the real issue. Through my tears and my anger, I blurted out to God, "How can You call Yourself a good Father when right now You're making *me* look like a *bad* father?"

When it was all said and done, I wept for almost two

hours in my car on the side of the road. Then, around 3:30 a.m., I was finally able to whisper a single phrase: "Okay. I trust You." I started my car, drove back home, and went to bed.

The next morning was the last day we could pay Holly's school fees before she was not allowed to come back to school. Just after 9:00 a.m., feeling exhausted and holding back tears, I picked up the phone to call the school and let them know we could not pay what was due. As I dialed the number, I felt the small whisper from the Holy Spirit say, *Log in and check your bank balance.*

Check my bank balance? I was indignant. *Just when I thought I couldn't be any more disappointed, now You want to rub it in my face?*

Just as the receptionist answered the phone, I heard that gentle whisper again: *Log in and check your bank balance.*

I hung up the phone before I could speak a word. This time I responded to the Spirit out loud: "How dare You ask me to do this! I *know* how much money is in my bank—nothing but a few dollars!" I was so mad I walked around for a few minutes to cool down before I made a third attempt to call the school.

"Hello," I heard the receptionist once again.

"Hello," I said. "I'd like to speak with someone regarding my daughter's school fees."

"One moment," she responded. And as she placed

the call on hold, again I heard the whisper of God's voice beckon to me: *Log in and check your bank balance!*

All of a sudden I realized God wasn't trying to humiliate me. He was *inviting* me to see something. I hung up the phone and rushed to my computer, fumbling to log in. And to my astonishment, I found that our bank account contained the exact amount we needed to pay not only Holly's school fees but every other outstanding bill as well—almost to the dollar.

What was even more incredible was that the money had been deposited overnight, right about the time I had uttered the words, "Okay. I trust You." There was barely a soul who knew our financial situation, and none who could have organized for that money to be deposited at exactly that time.

We had experienced a miracle—an amazing picture of what can happen when God's people sow faith and allow Him to produce a blessing.

WALKING IN FAITH

As amazing as it felt to hear Henry's story, God wasn't done teaching our family about the value of sowing in faith rather than attempting to reap a harvest on our own.

That Sunday as we sat in church, I felt the Lord impress upon my heart the command to sow every cent I had in my wallet when the bucket for tithes and offerings came around. Normally this was an easy command to obey, but that day it felt like a crazy move. Henry and I had just paid off our debts, but we had nothing left in our bank account. So if I gave my cash away, we would have nothing for another week before my paycheck hit.

As I pulled out every bit of cash I had, Henry leaned over and asked what I was doing. I said, "God told me to give everything."

I had never been in this position before, and it was frightening. But I also felt an overwhelming sense of peace. When Henry saw my tears, he pulled out the last $20 in his pocket, and we dropped everything we had into that offering bucket. I can remember feeling grateful for the knowledge that God was with us, and grateful that we had each other to hold.

Our couple's mantra since we began dating has always been a line from our favorite movie: "Me, you, five bucks, and a cup of coffee." That's all we needed. Yet there we were: me, Henry, no five bucks, and no cup of coffee in sight.

That night as we settled onto the couch to unwind, we received a text that said, "Go check your mailbox." We thought it was random. Henry couldn't believe it when he opened the mailbox and found an envelope inside with $200 cash. What on earth? He came bounding inside, wide-eyed, and showed me what he'd found. We could hardly contain our excitement! We ran around the house crying happy tears as we recognized the Father's miraculous provision once again.

Our God had provided for our every need. From that moment and over the next two years, God supernaturally replaced every single dollar that was taken from us by the unjust situation related to Henry's work and the dissolving of the band back in the United States. The money came in wads of cash in envelopes in our mailbox, checks for thousands of dollars from people we had never met, anonymous deposits in our bank account—miracle after miracle after miracle.

And then one day it stopped. We knew it wasn't really the *end*. It was the beginning of a new way of "walking in faith."

God moves in the opposite realm to our natural mind-set. It's natural for us to focus on reaping and harvesting—the world is all about the rewards and achievements we can earn through our own efforts. But when we sow in faith and place our trust in God, He really does open the windows of heaven and pour out blessings over our lives.

I love that my husband chose to sow instead of sue when he'd been wronged. Instead of fighting in the natural realm, we gave up control to the One who fights for us.

Learning how to trust God when there was nothing in our bank account developed our faith muscles and taught us that God is the God of the impossible. With Him there is no lack, and if we choose to live according to His kingdom principles, our lives will be blessed.

I truly believe Henry and I never would have had the courage or faith to move halfway around the world and see what God has done in these short few years here at The Belonging Co. if we hadn't learned how to yield in the hardest moments and utter that one phrase over and over: "Okay. I trust You."

DON'T GIVE UP!

I love these exhortations from the apostle Paul:

> Do not be deceived: God cannot be mocked. A man reaps what
> he sows. Whoever sows to please their flesh, from the flesh will
> reap destruction; whoever sows to please the Spirit, from the
> Spirit will reap eternal life. Let us not become weary in doing
> good, for at the proper time we will reap a harvest if we do not
> give up. Therefore, as we have opportunity, let us do good to all
> people, especially those who belong to the family of believers.
> (Gal. 6:7–10)

God is faithful and true. His Word cannot return void. He will
do what He promises. But we still need to be faithful—and sometimes we need to wait for His timing.

Sadly, there are many times when we give up right before we
have the chance to reap a miracle. The more difficult our circumstances, the harder it can be to trust God's plan. The more pain we
feel, the harder it can be to sow in faith. That's when we're in danger
of sowing to please the flesh, rather than to please the Spirit.

Don't give up! Don't grow weary in doing good!

If you're in a difficult time even now, resist the urge to find a
solution in your own strength. Reject the forces of this world that
push you to focus on what *you* need and everything *you* deserve
rather than the harvest *God* is preparing for you. Those forces only
lead to destruction.

God has promised that you will reap a harvest at the appointed time. What seems like the complete opposite thing to do in the natural may be exactly what needs to be done. God's ways are higher than our ways, and His thoughts are greater than our thoughts.

Henry and I have witnessed God's good ways over and over in our lives. And we love the beautiful reality that God gets the glory every time we share our stories of sowing and reaping. Those stories stir faith within the hearts of those who hear, whether they are following Christ or not. This principle of sowing and reaping works for the believer and the nonbeliever.

Remember: you will reap what you sow. So choose to sow faith rather than your own effort. Choose to sow according to the Spirit so that you can reap the abundance and joy God has planned for you.

CHALLENGE

What is God asking you to sow in faith? Take a step today and ask God what He would have you sow into. Keep a record of how you've sown and watch God be faithful with the harvest He will bring about.

EIGHTEEN

FEAR
VS.
FAITH

So do not fear, for I am with you; do not be dismayed,
for I am your God. I will strengthen you and help you;
I will uphold you with my righteous right hand.

—Isaiah 41:10

Fear is rampant in our generation. It torments and paralyzes those who believe that there is no way out. One of the greatest joys of being a pastor is counseling people from all walks of life and seeing them freed of this negative spirit. Their lives radically change as God reveals to them His power and they see how faith in Him can move the largest mountains.

Each and every one of us has this same power available to us to overcome fear. Jesus has given us the authority to speak to our mountains and see them removed. But it takes faith.

Faith is not just a theory; it is a weapon against the Enemy. So how does he strike back? He uses fear as a thief to steal our hope. That loss of hope makes us feel as if God has forsaken us. Yet God has said that we only need faith the size of a mustard seed to be able to speak to our mountain and tell it to move, because nothing is impossible for God (Matt. 17:20–21).

CAMERON'S STORY

Problems the size of mountains can come out of nowhere. And adversity is no respecter of people, so we need to be ready and equipped in how to overcome. I have asked another of my dear friends to share her story of facing seemingly impossible mountains. As you read, remember what the Scriptures tell us: nothing is impossible for our God!

In March of 2011, I gave birth to a beautiful baby girl. I fell head over heels in love with my petite little princess with sapphire blue eyes. Shortly after Elise's first birthday, after concern over some motor skill delays, my husband, James, and I were given the shocking news that she had some brain damage. Apparently, at some point when she was in utero, she was without oxygen, and it caused some white-matter damage in the back of her brain.

I hadn't been sick or unconscious while I was pregnant. It was simply considered an unknown injury, and they couldn't tell us concretely what her brain damage would mean for her future. I was heartbroken and scared but resolutely began a journey of therapy with my precious daughter. We landed at a place called High Hopes, where Elise would receive physical, speech, and occupational therapy.

That season was a lonely one; none of my friends had ever had to deal with anything like this with their babies. It was a sad and unsettling time for me because I had prayed over my little one since the moment I knew I was pregnant. How on earth could this have happened? Where was God in all of this?

During that wilderness season, I was given a book written by Charles Capps called *God's Creative Power*. It's a book about how faith comes from hearing and the power of our words. The book deeply resonated with me, and as a result I began writing scriptures on index cards and putting them all over my kitchen. I would read the verses over my girl while she ate her meals and snack throughout the day.

Pretty soon I got used to the sound of my own voice, and the power of God's words spoken from my lips started to shift things in me. I started to feel hope. I began combing Scripture for stories of healing and started coupling that time in God's Word by speaking God's promises out loud. Just like with Elise's therapy, slowly but surely, things started changing. I felt like God was saying to me, *Don't judge the future based on the present; leave room for the miraculous.*

It's amazing how the seeds for our future can come from the places of our greatest pain and disappointment. My daughter's occupational therapist and I became friends, and from that relationship came two different life-altering paths.

I am a songwriter, and so it was interesting to learn that her husband was a producer. We began collaborating together, which opened up some new opportunities for me professionally. She also invited me to a Bible study that was hosted by two Australians, Alex and Henry Seeley.

It was my pastor, Alex Seeley, who helped me begin to make sense of the tragedy in my life. She reminded me of a parable in the Bible that told of an enemy who came in at night and sowed weeds in with the tares of wheat. God allowed the weeds to grow for a time, but then there was a reckoning. At the time of harvest, the servant separated the wheat from the weeds and threw the weeds into the fire.

The takeaway from that story for me was that God was not the one who stole my daughter's breath in utero. The Enemy did. That hit hard. I have an Enemy. I knew the Bible tells us we wrestle not with flesh and blood but with rulers and principalities of darkness (Eph. 6:12). I knew who the Devil was and his part of the story. I guess I had always wanted to focus on Jesus and His grace and love for me. Now here I was, face-to-face with the reality of my Enemy and his attack on my daughter's life. I knew Jesus was strong enough to overcome him—I just wasn't sure if I was.

Here lies the key to my shift in that season. The more I started to focus on Jesus, the less fear I had of the Enemy and what he could do. The more I heard myself pray, the more I read about who God was and wasn't, and the more I spent time with Him in all my emotional states, the more my perspective and identity changed. God began to whisper to me that I was a warrior. Slowly, ever so slowly, I began to believe Him. My fear was being changed into faith.

I thought Elise's brain damage was the big mountain in my life, but I was wrong. When my daughter was three, in November of 2014, I noticed some abnormal bruising all over her body. Later that night Elise started vomiting, so first thing in the morning we were at the ER. After a blood test, we were quickly admitted and she was given two blood transfusions on arrival.

They initially thought she had leukemia, but sadly the truth turned out to be even more painful. We discovered a week into our hospital stay that Elise has an ultrarare disease called atypical hemolytic uremic syndrome (aHUS). We were the first pediatric case ever in Nashville. Providentially, there was another little girl from Kentucky who had been treated at our hospital, and so they were able to recognize my daughter's symptoms.

We discovered there was only one treatment for this incredibly rare disease: a brand-new drug that had been approved by the FDA in September of 2011, the same year my daughter was born.

This drug was the most expensive drug in the world at the time, and we had to sign a horrible document that said if our insurance couldn't cover the cost of the medication, then the hospital could only afford to give it to her for maybe two years tops. Can you imagine? I was like, "Then what? She dies?" I had no idea at the time there were other resources that would never have let that happen, but in the moment, everything came crashing down and I almost went under. Fear tried to take hold of me again, but even stronger than before.

I remember watching that medicine drip into my daughter's IV late that night, so afraid of what might happen next. Elise was so weak and bloated and couldn't open her eyes. The pressure of this being the only treatment available and the fear that it might not work paralyzed me. I told God, *If the Enemy is like a roaring lion roaming about seeking whom he can devour, then I definitely feel hunted! And it's like he has me in his jaws, just limp prey.*

I was weak and fearful. In my flesh, I wanted to curl up in a ball and weep in despair, but what happened next was a revelation that changed the course of my life. Almost audibly, I heard God say to me, *Cameron, I am the Lion of Judah, and I can outhunt what hunts you! In fact, I'm going to teach you how to hunt him. Get up and go take authority as her mom. You speak to that mountain in the same way you spoke to Elise's brain damage mountain.*

I told the Lord, *I don't even know what to pray.*

He said, *Go pray the Lord's Prayer: "Thy kingdom come, thy will be done." My perfect will is her perfect healing.* The Lord was with me in the valley of the shadow of death, and without me realizing it, He had prepped me for battle!

I tearfully got up and whispered into my daughter's ear and prayed over her. From that point on, the turnaround began. Praise God our daughter regained 100 percent kidney function and all her blood levels returned to normal! Elise would begin a biweekly infusion, and that became our new normal. I continued to write music, but now from a warrior stance. I wanted to take back enemy territory.

AHUS is considered a genetic disease, and our genetic testing revealed my husband was the carrier. In the back of my mind, I knew it was possible for him to manifest the disease, but I prayed he never would. Genetics are interesting because people can have genetic mutations for things but never have a "trigger" that wakes up the disease.

Then the unthinkable happened—my husband got sick. Looking back, it's amazing how similar but different my husband's aHUS onset experience was. We recognized the symptoms when he started manifesting them, and James ended up admitting himself into the ER. He was able to walk in and tell them about his genetic mutation, what blood tests to run, and what to look for, and ultimately to give them a diagnosis. He arrived at the ER in kidney failure with 20 percent kidney function.

We say that Elise saved my husband's life. Because of her, we were educated and armed and ready for the fight. James was able to get on the same life-saving drug and spent only a week in the hospital. Our daughter spent fifteen days. He rebounded to 100 percent kidney function, and now he is Elise's biweekly infusion buddy.

When James got sick, I felt the tsunami of fear and panic crash over me like before. I just found my footing much faster this time. God had led me through the valley of the shadow of death with Elise and proven that He would not leave us. So I waged war like I did with Elise. I slung God's promises at the Enemy and released all our prayer warriors to lay siege with us. We rallied the troops and again the Enemy retreated. I like to say the Enemy will regret the day he came for my family and me. What the Enemy meant for evil, God is now using for great good.

Having an ultrarare disease has taken us to places we never dreamed. We spoke at a sales conference for the pharmaceutical company that makes our drug, and I have been able to perform and speak at various charity galas and events raising awareness for our disease and a new bill.

My husband's and daughter's stories have a much bigger purpose than just being about them. My journey from fear to faith was not just about my family's mountains. I'm honored to now bear witness to a much bigger story. A story of God's faithfulness and provision and "the good-ness of the LORD in the land of the living" (Ps. 27:13). A story of overcoming. It's because of my time in darkness that I discovered who I was, that I have not been given a spirit of fear but of power, love, and a sound mind.

F.E.A.R.—FALSE EVIDENCE APPEARING REAL

Fear is a powerful and overwhelming feeling induced by perceived danger. It has the power to paralyze the best of us and can cause us to shut down. Fear can make us become completely irrational, which can then turn into a phobia that affects our entire life. But 2 Timothy 1:7 says, "For God has not given us a spirit of fear and timidity, but of power, love, and self-discipline" (NLT).

Fear is the opposite of faith. Fear causes us to shrink back from a situation, but faith enables us to move toward Jesus. We may still feel afraid, but we should not allow fear to cripple us because with God we can overcome any situation that is threatening to overwhelm us. Though we face real challenges, we serve a God who is victorious. With Him we have the power to overcome anything that comes our way. Even though we face real challenges, we serve a God who is victorious. We too can access the power to overcome anything that comes our way.

Someone once stated that F.E.A.R. as an acronym stands for "false evidence appearing real." We are so often afraid of things that have never even happened, or we are afraid because of things that have happened to us in the past.

However, even though you may be faced with a real tragedy, you are not to be overwhelmed. Instead, you are to be convinced of the truth of God's Word. When I was diagnosed with infertility for instance, the facts were that my body could not get pregnant. I did not live in denial, but I chose to stand on the truth that God could heal my body, pointing to the scripture that says, "By His stripes we are healed" (Isa. 53:5 NKJV). It wasn't that I thought I may be healed, or I hoped to be healed. I stood on the truth that I *was* healed. If Jesus' death and resurrection healed my spiritual condition, it could also have the power to heal my physical condition.

Many of us lower our theology to fit our circumstances, but instead, we need to raise our circumstances to the truth of God's Word. I still went to the doctor and followed the plan they had for me, but I also petitioned heaven for a miracle to be appropriated to my body. I fought that spiritual battle for two years and encountered God in a way that let me know He is the great healer.

I was fully convinced of His power to heal me. I walked by faith, not fear, over what was happening. I pressed in with prayer and thanksgiving and brought my requests to the One who had the power to answer them. The peace of God that transcends all understanding did guard my heart and mind in Christ Jesus, just as Philippians 4:6–7 says.

I love the idea that fear is based on *false* evidence, because our faith is placed in *real* evidence. In John 14:6, God literally proclaims

Himself to be *the truth*. The world is prone to become anxious and fearful when they do not have a power greater than themselves to depend on. When they have run out of options and exhausted all manner of help, they panic. But this is where the people of faith can call upon a faithful God who says we need not fear.

Faith comes by hearing and reading the Word of God and making an agreement with it. Declare that truth over your life. This exercises your faith muscle.

This is a weapon of warfare many people are unaware of. They get overwhelmed by fear and take themselves out of the fight, but we are not a people who shrink back. Instead, we advance forward toward enemy lines with the sword of the Word of God and the shield of faith, knowing that the battle is the Lord's.

No one else can do this for you. You need to decide, "I will believe that my God is for me and that He is not finished yet. So I will continue to trust in His nature and wait patiently for Him to answer my prayer." Even if your prayer does not get answered on this side of eternity, you need to know that God is good regardless of the outcome. We must continue to fight the fight of faith and trust that God will accomplish His plan for our lives in His timing, and in ways that we may not expect.

If you are overcome by fear, I am here to tell you that you have the power in Christ to overcome it. You do not have to live with this spirit over you. Your circumstances may not change for a season while you are waiting for the miracle, but *you* will change for the better. Something inside you will stand up and cause you to be the person who lives by faith and not by sight.

Remember, the world is watching how you face every situation. They are hoping that the God we serve is who He says He is. The more we fix our eyes on Jesus, who is love and truth, the less fear we will have. We will behold Him to be the God He says He is.

CHALLENGE

If you are experiencing fear right now, allow the fullness of the love of God to permeate every part of your heart. Repent for coming into agreement with the spirit of fear. Declare God's truth over your heart and over your situation in order to debunk "false evidence appearing real." Speak to your mountain with bold faith and command it to move. Believe until you see a breakthrough.

NINETEEN

PRIDE VS. HUMILITY

God opposes the proud but shows favor to the humble.

—1 Peter 5:5

In my early twenties, I could be at times critical, judgmental, and exclusive. I cared about what people thought about me and tried very hard to be noticed by the right people. You know, like the ones who could open doors for me. The people who would drop my name and connect me with others who could help propel me into my destiny. I would compare myself to others who were in the same area of leadership and think I could do it better than they could. Oh my word! I am cringing as I write this. At the end of the day, though I had a soft heart, my need for validation was crippling me. I was so bent on proving myself that I found myself doing and saying things I am not proud of today.

One day I remember reading Philippians 2:1–30 during a season when I was trying so hard to have my dreams realized. I was unprepared for how this passage of Scripture was about to wreck me to the core of my being. It was the first time I had seen the humility of Christ in its raw truth. Verses 3–8 say:

> Do nothing out of selfish ambition or vain conceit. Rather, in humility value others above yourselves, not looking to your own interests but each of you to the interests of the others.
>
> In your relationships with one another, have the same mindset as Christ Jesus:
>
> Who, being in the very nature God,
> > did not consider equality with God
> something to be used to his own advantage;
> rather, he made himself nothing
> > by taking the very nature of a servant,
> > being made in human likeness.
> And being found in appearance as a man,
> > he humbled himself
> > by becoming obedient to death—
> > > even death on a cross!

This is God we are talking about! Not some prophet who claims to be God. This is the Creator of the universe and all mankind, and

He chose to humble Himself and obey God. He walked in humility, not having to prove Himself to anyone.

Humility comes from a place of security, where you know who you are and you have no need to be validated by anyone else.

SLOW AND STEADY WINS THE RACE

If I could speak to my twenty-year-old self, I would take her out for a cup of coffee and remind her of one of Aesop's Fables called "The Tortoise and the Hare." You might remember it from your own childhood.

There was once a speedy hare who bragged about how fast he could run. Tired of hearing him boast, Slow and Steady, the tortoise, challenged him to race. All the animals in the forest gathered to watch.

Hare ran down the road for a while and then paused to rest. He looked back at Slow and Steady and cried out, "How do you expect to win this race when you are walking along at your slow, slow pace?"

Hare stretched himself out alongside the road and fell asleep, thinking, "There is plenty of time to relax."

Slow and Steady walked and walked. He never, ever stopped until he came to the finish line.

The animals who were watching cheered so loudly for Tortoise, they woke up Hare.

Hare stretched and yawned and began to run again, but it was too late. Tortoise was over the line.

After that, Hare always reminded himself, "Don't brag about your lightning pace, for Slow and Steady won the race!"[1]

My twenty-year-old self needed to read those words every day. "Don't brag about your lightning pace, for slow and steady wins the race."

Can you imagine a world where people are not striving to be known but know who they are and are comfortable with themselves? Where people accomplish what has been assigned to them by God? A world where ambition and rivalry cease because we all have an understanding of our place in the world?

We all have a destiny and a purpose. Yet we live in a world where who we are associated with makes us feel better about ourselves. We are so ambitious and driven, yet so insecure. Because of that insecurity, we feel as though we have to prove ourselves, pushing people out of our way in the process.

We are the hare, focused on our speed and relying on our innate gifts to get us ahead. But when we run our race in this posture of pride, we earn medals of destruction. In contrast, humility sets us up securely to run our races well.

My husband runs his race this way. He is one of the most humble men I have ever met. He has been given an immeasurable number

---

1 "The Tortoise and the Hare," Story Library, http://www.storyarts.org/library/aesops/stories/tortoise.html.

of talents and gifts, and yet I have never seen him promote himself, name-drop, or push anyone else aside to fulfill his dreams. Others usually speak of his résumé. What he has achieved in the short time he has been alive is nothing short of awe-inspiring. But he constantly serves others, and he never tells people what he has accomplished.

I remember a time when we were in a season of hiddenness and our character was being tested. (Actually, where *my* character was being tested!) Some of our friends were being noted for their incredible achievements and seeing their dreams unfold in the public eye. When we were around these amazing people, everything inside of me would want Henry to promote himself. I would wish someone would ask an applicable question so that we could "conveniently" talk about what Henry was working on. But when the time came, and it did on more than one occasion, Henry would keep quiet. I was like, "What? Could you please just drop a few hints so we can be included in this group and get connected?" Yet Henry wouldn't say anything. It would infuriate me because I would want to run ahead and make something happen, but Henry would constantly challenge me, reminding me that it is God who promotes and we just needed to be slow and steady. God would work out the rest.

Proverbs 27:2 says, "Let someone else praise you, and not your own mouth; an outsider, and not your own lips." No one likes a name-dropper anyway, especially one who promotes themselves.

Henry has taught me so much in our walk of faith, but one of the greatest is this concept of being consistently faithful. I can really trust God to guide our steps and lead us into the right place at the right time without the need to highlight ourselves. God wants us to have a humble heart, satisfied to do the everyday, mundane assignments with excellence rather than be one who runs ahead for a season of preemptive or false highlights.

Being humble means thinking of yourself less. It's when you will do whatever job is needed, no matter who you are or where you are, and not for the accolades. It is the posture that demonstrates servanthood to Jesus and gives Him the glory. Humility knows it is not about our name in lights, but about His light that shines through us. My friend Christine Caine says it like this: "We are not meant to be costars with Christ; we are called to be co-laborers with Christ."

THE ENEMY OF PRIDE

We are all called to run the race marked out for us, but some of us run as if we were competing against one another. We don't realize we are on the same team. Our rival or competitor is not the person in the lane to the left or right of us! Our rival is the Enemy. And pride has ruined him.

Pride caused Lucifer to fall from heaven. Ezekiel 28 describes what pride cost him: "You were blameless in your ways from the day you were created till wickedness was found in you. . . . Your heart became proud on account of your beauty, and you corrupted your wisdom because of your splendor. So I [the Lord God] threw you to the earth; I made a spectacle of you before kings" (vv. 15, 17).

Pride robbed Lucifer of the good he had. He became so obsessed with his own beauty and power that he pitted himself against God, and he became desirous of the glory and power that truly belonged to the Lord. And as we know, this posture doesn't end well. He lost his place and position of heavenly authority, as indicated in Luke 10:18: "Satan [fell] like lightning from heaven." And the power he *did* have became completely corrupt. Finally, we know his future will end in utter destruction in the lake of fire (Matt. 25:41).

Harsh and horrific, I know. But God hates pride (Prov. 8:13). Humility operates in the opposite spirit. Rather than competing with one another or trying to be like God, we know our position in Christ and we are secure in it. Humility honors and freely worships who God is, content to be made in His image.

Humility is not concerned with one's own importance, even when it comes to what we *do* for God. This is another way pride rears its ugly head and is a ploy of Satan. When Jesus was in the wilderness at the start of His ministry, Satan wanted Him to prove Himself when he tempted Him. But Jesus did not need to prove Himself to Satan or anyone else. He knew who He was. God the Father had just affirmed to the world that He was His Son at His baptism. We are often tempted to want others to know how important we are. But as long as God knows our name, we can be confident that our reputation will go before us.

THE HUMBLE ARE GIVEN GRACE

One time I was invited to attend the video taping of a curriculum series on one of the Gospels. The speaker and I had become instant friends after a chance meeting on a flight home to Nashville.

I arrived late and discovered that there was only one seat remaining—right in front of the podium where my friend was about to speak. I was not dressed for the occasion of a video recording, but not wanting to miss out, I hustled my way to the last remaining seat and waited for the Bible study to commence. My friend was still getting camera ready in the back while the audience chatted with one another, waiting for it to begin. But no one was talking to me.

I felt a little uncomfortable but remained seated. A few minutes later, a gentleman came up to me and asked me politely if I would move seats. I said yes, and he ushered me to the back corner of the room. I was actually relieved that I was not front and center, but as I looked down at my outfit and then looked around at all the other ladies (who still weren't talking to me), it hit me. *Oh! I don't fit in here.*

I was wearing ripped jeans and a leather jacket and my hair was in a tussled topknot. My pride was a little hurt as I sat in silence—though my internal dialogue was having a full-on discussion as to whether I should get up and leave or stay. Of course, because of my love for my friend, I decided to stay and humble myself and remain in the back corner.

My friend made her way to the podium to begin. As she looked around the room and made eye contact with me, she gasped with excitement and then did something that scared me half to death. She introduced me and asked if I would pray over the Bible study, in front of all these women. They immediately turned to me and welcomed me, even going so far as to clap and cheer. I prayed with all my heart. God whispered to me in that moment that I would never have to prove myself or require any validation from anyone.

That as I humbled myself to serve others, He would make a way for me at the appointed time.

Imagine if my pride had gotten the better of me and I'd started spouting off about who I was and how I knew my friend. That would have been ugly. But as I humbled myself, honored the authority around me, and submitted to the request of doing what others saw fit to do, God spoke on my behalf. I have actually now become wonderful friends with some of the other women who were there, even though we are from different denominations and churches.

This is a good story, and the principle remains true. Those who humble themselves will be given grace and lifted up at the appointed time. Those who are full of pride will fall down in the long run.

In humility, Jesus served mankind and died for our sins. Then He was lifted up at the appointed time and made the name that is above every name. He went low, and God lifted Him high. It was never about Jesus becoming famous; it was always about Jesus doing what the Father asked. He was obedient unto death.

CHALLENGE

Ask the Lord to reveal to you if there is any pride in your heart. If there is, repent and choose to humble yourself in the presence of God. When you feel pride rising up or feel the need to be validated, just close your mouth. God will give grace to the humble (1 Peter 5:6). Move in the opposite spirit by honoring those around you and serving them well. Watch God raise you up at the appointed time.

TWENTY

AWARDS VS. CROWNS

"So when you give to the needy, do not announce it with
trumpets, as the hypocrites do in the synagogues and
on the streets, to be honored by others. Truly I tell you,
they have received their reward in full."

—Matthew 6:2

Human nature loves to be validated and applauded for doing good
works. Beginning in childhood we are awarded for good behavior and
for achieving certain goals. We champion the hero and strive for trophies
and physical awards that bring us accolades and notoriety, but we forget
that our lives are so much more than collecting statues and medals.

Our lives continue on in eternity, and what we do here on earth holds much weight in the eternal. Whatever is temporal does not go with us into eternity. Whatever is done God's way, according to the upside-down kingdom, is noted within the heavenly kingdom that has no end. This kingdom lifestyle of moving in the opposite realm begins when we invite Jesus into our lives, but it does not end when we die. We continue living in heaven.

According to 1 Corinthians 3:12–15, what we do here on earth will be revealed and tested through fire. Either it will be burned up as wood, hay, and stubble, or it will last forever. The latter is what we take into eternity with us. It's also what we get to give back to God when we see Him face-to-face just like the twenty-four elders do in Revelation 4:10–11: "The twenty-four elders fall down before him who sits on the throne and worship him who lives for ever and ever. They lay their crowns before the throne and say: 'You are worthy, our Lord and God, to receive glory and honor and power, for you created all things, and by your will they were created and have their being.'"

What a moment to look forward to. Can you imagine the day when we also get to cast our crowns before the throne of God and honor Him for being the name that is above every other name?

SEEK FIRST HIS KINGDOM AND ALL THESE THINGS ARE ADDED

As you now know, my husband, Henry, has been a music producer and mix engineer for many years. His dream ever since he was a toddler was to become a professional musician. That's all he ever wanted to do, and by God's grace he has been able to do it since he was nineteen years old.

He had great success in being a worship leader, producer, and mix engineer for an incredible movement in Australia, so when we moved to America, we automatically assumed he would continue to do this full-time. We expected God to open more opportunities that would extend his music career.

After a couple of years in Nashville, Henry was working with many artists and worship teams mixing and producing albums. Life was good. In the natural, this pathway made sense to us. However, things started to shift when God presented us with the idea that the gathering in our basement was to be a church and that we would pastor it. Henry began to wrestle with how he was going to fulfill his music career and do what God was asking him to do in pastoring these people. Henry found himself at a crossroads. Shepherding one hundred people, and doing it well, didn't permit him the time to fully continue in music the way he had been.

One night he was mixing a record when one of our people who was out on tour was having a hard time. Pastoring over the phone meant that Henry wasn't able to fully concentrate on finishing the album. After the call, in his own prayer time with the Lord, Henry asked the question, *Why are You asking me to do this when it was never part of my dream?*

His prayer thoughts continued, *How am I going to do all of this?* because at the time the church was not paying us to lead them. We had bills to pay, and the only income we had was from his music production.

At that moment Henry felt God lead him to a scripture in 1 Peter 5:2–4:

> Be shepherds of God's flock that is under your care, watching over them—not because you must, but because you are willing, as God wants you to be; not pursuing dishonest gain, but eager to serve; not lording it over those entrusted to you, but being examples to the flock. And when the Chief Shepherd appears, you will receive the crown of glory that will never fade away.

Henry felt God ask him to shepherd the flock within his reach. God wasn't demanding it of Henry, but was asking us to look after these people. Henry felt so overwhelmed in that moment by the love of God for the people who had become this body. He chose to surrender his agenda and dreams and walk the narrow road of obedience. It was as if he was laying down the future of receiving anything that pertained to music. Shepherding these musicians gathered in our basement didn't feel as glamorous as Henry getting to actually work in music, but he obeyed.

Ironically, the following two years were the busiest season for Henry. He was not only pastoring the men and women at The Belonging Co., but he had booked more work than ever as a producer and engineer. He barely slept for over two years. He worked on music through the early hours of the morning, and during the day he helped pastor and lead this new church. I don't know too many successful musicians who would lay down their status and the work they love to do to pastor a bunch of misfit musicians who were traveling the world doing the very thing Henry loves to do.

During this incredibly busy time, Henry found himself mix engineering a record for a very talented artist. He worked hard to finish the project with excellence. If this was how God wanted his life to look, even if it meant sleepless nights, he would do it.

After the record was completed, it was nominated for a Grammy. This meant Henry was also up for winning a Grammy as best mix engineer for the project.

He could not believe his ears when he received the phone call because winning a Grammy was his dream as a young boy. In the music world's eyes, winning a Grammy is the pinnacle of awards. Winning this little gold statue means world-renowned favor in your field of expertise.

When it came time to attend the Grammy award show in Los Angeles, we made our way down the red carpet. It was nothing like I imagined it to be. Everything felt as if it were moving in slow motion. Amid the chaos of beautifully dressed celebrities and media personnel trying to get into the arena and fans and paparazzi shouting to get the attention of the stars, I heard a sound I had never heard before.

It wasn't a physical sound; it was more like I could hear the chatter of self-talk going on all around me. It was as though hundreds of people were talking to themselves internally and the sound was deafening. Screams of "Pick me," "Notice me," and "Look at me" filled my head. It continued with things like, "Am I good enough?" and, "Am I pretty enough?" It was the sound of striving to be known. And it grieved my heart as I saw so many people who didn't understand the value of the eternal and were desperate for the temporal treasures of this world's value system and its validation.

As we were being herded like cattle through the red carpet tunnel, I kept my head down and walked into the arena. We sat down and began to watch the show. Henry's category was announced near the end. When the person opened the envelope and announced the winning name of the record, we couldn't believe our ears. The album won Best Gospel Album, which also meant Henry won! He won a Grammy!

After all the outbursts of joy and congratulatory texts blew up our phones, we left the arena and went to eat a burger and fries. Nothing had really changed. We felt the same as we did the moment before he won. It almost felt anticlimactic. Then Henry said something so profound. He said, "Wow, if this is what people strive to attain their whole lives, it feels really empty." We actually left early that night and got on a plane for home the next day, returning to our normal but beautiful life of pastoring The Belonging Co.

It was so amazing to us to think about how many people strive for this man-made statue that now sits on our bookshelf and needs to be dusted every week along with the other ornaments. It's great, absolutely, but not lasting. This statue will not go to heaven with Henry. The award will not matter on the other side of eternity. It's what we do in the unseen that will be rewarded by God.

AWARDS THAT NEVER FADE AWAY

Let's look again at 1 Corinthians 3:12–15 to get a better idea of what our earthly works accomplish.

> If anyone builds on this foundation using gold, silver, costly stones, wood, hay or straw, their work will be shown for what it is, because the Day will bring it to light. It will be revealed with fire, and the fire will test the quality of each person's work. If what has been built survives, the builder will receive a reward. If it is burned up, the builder will suffer loss but yet will be saved— even though only as one escaping through the flames.

When we first come to know Christ and enter this new kingdom realm, it is just the beginning of the race marked out for us. At the end of the race, there will be a test as to whether there was any value in what we did on earth. Our motives will be tested, our hearts will be sifted, and our deeds will be judged. If we are saved but do nothing within the kingdom and live according to our flesh until we die, we will not lose our salvation. We will enter heaven, but we will lose our reward. But if there is value to what we did on earth, then we will receive the lasting reward of a crown.

I often think of this in regard to the awards and accolades we receive while on earth. They'll amount to nothing on the other side of eternity, so I want to make sure that what I ultimately accomplish on earth lasts forever. I want to achieve a reward that never fades away.

Again, this is the upside-down kingdom way of thinking that is so counter to our flesh. We want the awards and the fame now, but God tells us not to store up treasures here, where moth and rust will destroy them. He instructs us instead to store up treasures in heaven where they will not fade away. You may not get a physical award this side of eternity, but you will receive a crown that you will be able to place at the feet of Jesus in heaven. What an honor it will be to lay our crowns before Him. When we see Jesus face-to-face, we'll know even more that He is the only one truly worthy of all honor and worship. I imagine we'll lay prostrate before Him, our crowns clinking together as they hit the ground in surrender.

THE CROWNS OF LASTING REWARD

Let's take a look at four specific crowns mentioned in the Bible as rewards and find out how to obtain them as we live out the opposite life.

1. The Crown of Righteousness

For I am already being poured out like a drink offering, and the time for my departure is near. I have fought the good fight, I have finished the race, I have kept the faith. Now there is in store for me the crown of righteousness, which the Lord, the righteous Judge, will award to me on that day—and not only to me, but also to all who have longed for his appearing. (2 Tim. 4:6–8)

The crown of righteousness has little to do with our salvation. We will all arrive in eternity if we call on the name of the Lord, because salvation is a gift. Our salvation has been settled, and our names have been written in the Lamb's Book of Life. Whether you receive the crown of righteousness, however, depends on how you run your race here. Righteousness is the right way of doing life according to God's kingdom principles.

We can be saved, but we can still choose to live a life not pleasing to God. The following are examples of Christians who will not receive the crown of righteousness: those who think it's okay to cheat and tell little white lies, who take revenge and cause division and strife among the body, who choose to hold grudges, or who live an immoral lifestyle against the principles set out in Galatians 5. It is when we choose to do what is right in God's eyes, when no one is looking, that God takes notice and keeps record.

What we do matters, even the small things. Matthew 12:36–37 says, "But I tell you that everyone will have to give account on the day of judgment for every empty word they have spoken. For by your words you will be acquitted, and by your words you will be condemned." If we are being held accountable for our words, how much more are we going to be given a reward for doing good?

2. The Incorruptible Crown

Do you not know that in a race all the runners run, but only one gets the prize? Run in such a way as to get the prize. Everyone who competes in the games goes into strict training. They do it to get a crown that will not last, but we do it to get a crown that will last forever. (1 Cor. 9:24–25)

This crown is given to those who faithfully endure the race of serving God. It is given to those who have kept their eyes fixed on Jesus instead of being distracted with the things of this life. Professional athletes don't receive a gold medal by eating junk food and lying around on the couch all day watching TV, but instead they maintain intense training in order to be the best.

When we choose to live life on a consistent basis, running the race well God's way, we too will receive a crown, but one that is incorruptible. This crown is given to us when we choose to go the extra mile, when we choose to forgive, when we choose to lay down our lives for the cause of Christ, and when we choose to take the narrow road and follow Jesus, even when it doesn't make sense.

3. The Crown of Life

Do not be afraid of what you are about to suffer. I tell you, the devil will put some of you in prison to test you, and you will suffer persecution for ten days. Be faithful, even to the point of death, and I will give you life as your victor's crown. (Rev. 2:10)

This crown is also called "the martyr's crown." Jesus said that He will give this crown to those who endure hardships, testing, and trials through persecution and death for His sake. In John 12:25, Jesus says, "Anyone who loves their life will lose it, while anyone who hates their life in this world will keep it for eternal life." Again, the opposite mind-set is highlighted here, and those who lost their life for their faith will receive a lasting crown.

4. The Crown of Glory

> Be shepherds of God's flock that is under your care, watching over them—not because you must, but because you are willing, as God wants you to be; not pursuing dishonest gain, but eager to serve; not lording it over those entrusted to you, but being examples to the flock. And when the Chief Shepherd appears, you will receive the crown of glory that will never fade away. (1 Pet. 5:2–4)

This crown will be given to the faithful shepherds of God's flock who served consistently. This means all of us who have cared for the sheep, and it doesn't matter whether you were entrusted with one or thousands. It only matters that you served others faithfully. They shall receive a gift as a reward when they have finished the work and they will reign with Christ as kings on a throne of glory, wearing a crown of glory and enjoying the kingdom for all eternity. This crown of glory will be unfading, carrying with it honor, authority, and notoriety in the eyes of God. This crown will be given to those who were faithful to overcome and sustain the calling of God until the end.

THE BLESSINGS OF LIVING IN GOD'S UPSIDE-DOWN KINGDOM

Jesus is our greatest example in living a life that is opposite to seeking earthly treasures and crowns. He lived contrary to the natural.

He did what was right in the eyes of God and lived according to the ways of the kingdom of God. He was crowned on earth with thorns and surrendered His life as a sacrifice for us, but the story doesn't end there. He rose again and ascended to heaven, where He received the lasting crown of glory and honor.

I don't want to be empty-handed at the throne of God because I scraped into eternity with my salvation. I want to bring a gift to the King of kings. I want to honor Him with my life on earth. I want to run the race and fight the good fight of faith. I want Him to know that He has always been my prize. And most of all, I want to hear the words, "Well done, good and faithful servant!"

I do not believe we will feel any condemnation in Christ in heaven, but I think we will wish we had done more on this side of eternity. You see, we live with a temporal mind-set, when we should be living with an eternal mind-set from the moment we receive salvation. This earthly home is one we pass through until we reach eternity with Jesus. We will reign with Him forever, and I want to make sure that what He died for, I choose to live for.

Perhaps you will not see the justice you hoped for on this side of eternity. Perhaps you will have felt like you fought the good fight of faith and did not receive anything for it. Perhaps you will be the person who will remain in the shadows of the unseen while here on earth. But know this: our God is a just Judge. He will vindicate you and reward you for your faithful service. Justice will prevail, and God will honor those who have served Him.

Our faith in Christ boils down to one thing: Jesus is the only One worthy to be worshipped, and Jesus is the One we will honor for all eternity. At the end of the day, we are not deserving of anything because we all fall short of the glory of God. Salvation is the greatest gift that we should never take for granted. It is because of His great love for us that He stepped in to take our place and give us eternal life. It's because He chose to give everything up for me that I now choose to live wholeheartedly for Him.

When we look around us at the ways we could obtain this world's crowns, the opposite life may not seem appealing at first. Its ways may feel so contrary to where our flesh wants to go at times. But when we choose to do life God's way, we will see that His ways are so much better than ours. We will discover that living consistently according to the principles of His kingdom is the most fruitful and blessed way to live.

We will have wished we discovered the mystery sooner. And when we make our way to eternity, we will finally see that what we thought of as the upside-down kingdom of God here on earth has actually been the right way up the whole time. And it will be an absolute honor to cast our crowns at His feet and cry, "'Holy, holy, holy is the Lord God Almighty,' who was, and is, and is to come" (Rev. 4:8). Just thinking about this moment takes my breath away.

CHALLENGE

Your final challenge is this: Make a commitment to live every day with the opposite life in mind. When you face an issue that may cause you to react negatively, ask yourself, "What would Jesus do?"

Be quick to obey what He says, and if you do this consistently, I can promise that you will discover the mystery of living with power and abundance and rewards beyond anything you could ever hope or imagine!

May we *change* the world just like Jesus did by bringing heaven to earth.

ABOUT THE AUTHOR

ALEX SEELEY was born and raised in Australia and spent seventeen years pastoring there. It is also where she met and married her husband, Henry. After relocating to Nashville in 2012, they founded The Belonging Co., a church where they minister together to thousands of people each week. She is a passionate teacher of the Word with the unique ability to reveal how the Word of God is applicable to our everyday lives.

NOTES

NOTES

NOTES

THE
BELONGING
Co

After relocating to Nashville, TN, in April 2012, Henry and Alex Seeley began opening their home on Tuesday nights for people to worship, encounter God, and build genuine community in a city where people's personal and spiritual lives often succumb to the transient nature of "life on the road."

During their first meeting with just a handful of people, something profound happened—the presence of God filled the room and every person there had an encounter with God in a fresh and tangible way. Continuing to meet every other week, it only took a few months before their basement was at capacity and The Belonging Co. was born.

After two years of meeting together, The Belonging Co. now reaches over 3,000 people across Nashville and thousands online from all over the world. We can't put into words what God is doing, but we are sure about one thing: He is building His church and changing people's lives from the inside out.

We desire encounter over entertainment, intimacy over industry, presence over presentation, people over position—and most of all JESUS over everything.

WWW.THEBELONGING.CO

Please visit Alex at alexseeley.com to learn more about her, her ministry, and stay up to date with where she is speaking. You can also follow her on social media.

@alexseeley   @officialalexseeley   @alexseeley73

"*Tailor Made* is a powerful book and a must-read for every generation."
—Christine Caine, founder of A21 and Propel Women

"My friend Alex is a force! The inspiring words of *Tailor Made* will help you shed the limiting labels of your past and position you to draw near to our Master Tailor Father."
—Lisa Bevere, *New York Times* bestselling author

"I devoured this book and found myself wanting to read it again because of the impact of [Alex's] message."
—Danny Gokey, Grammy-nominated and Dove Award-winning artist

YOU'RE NOT ONE-SIZE-FITS-ALL.
YOUR DESIGNER KNOWS YOU'VE BEEN *TAILOR MADE*.

If you've ever wondered what God was thinking when He made you, or if you've wrestled with those big questions—"Why am I here?" "What's my purpose?"— then *Tailor Made* is for you.

In *Tailor Made*, Alex Seeley will help you recognize the wrong thinking and labels often brought on by generational patterns, insecurities, difficult circumstances, unforgiveness, and an inaccurate view of God and exchange them for the truth of who God created you to be.

Your labels don't have to define you. Be the original you were created to be.